A BEGINNER'S GUIDE
TO PEOPLE LEADERSHIP

on your
marks,
get set...
LEAD!

Anna Marshall

Acknowledgement of Country

I acknowledge the Australian Aboriginal and Torres Strait Islander peoples of this nation. I acknowledge the traditional custodians of the lands on which the members of the People Mastery team and our families live and love; the Bundjalung, Ngarigo, Ngunawal and Worimi peoples. We also acknowledge the traditional custodians of the lands where we connect with our clients. We pay our respects to ancestors and Elders, past and present. We deeply appreciate and honour Australian Aboriginal and Torres Strait Islander people's unique cultural and spiritual relationships to the land, waters and seas and their rich contribution to society.

A leadership haiku

Inspiring leaders
Foresee who we can become
And invest in us.

For Neve and Miles, for you dear reader, and for every other beginning leader out there.

May this be just the book you've been looking for.

First published in 2021 by Anna Marshall

A catalogue entry for this book is available from the National Library of Australia.

ISBN: 978-1-922553-30-0

Printed in Australia by McPherson's Printing
Project management and text design by Publish Central
Cover design by Peter Reardon

The paper this book is printed on is certified as environmentally friendly.

Disclaimer
The material in this publication is of the nature of general comment only, and does not
represent professional advice. It is not intended to provide specific guidance for particular
circumstances and it should not be relied on as the basis for any decision to take action or
not take action on any matter which it covers. Readers should obtain professional advice
where appropriate, before making any such decision. To the maximum extent permitted
by law, the author and publisher disclaim all responsibility and liability to any person,
arising directly or indirectly from any person taking or not taking action based on the
information in this publication.

Contents

Introduction

YOUR CHOICE

There are many people who have a responsibility for people leadership who have made the choice (consciously or unconsciously) to serve themselves rather than the people they lead. These people occupy CEO roles, team leader roles and everything in between. I'm sure you've spotted some of them along your way. Sadly, people who have made this choice are still too common in so many of today's organisations.

Early in my career I was working as a Human Resources Manager when I was called in by the then CEO for 'a chat'. He wasn't the most endearing man I'd ever met, and the feeling of dread was slowly rising in my stomach as I walked towards his office ...

'Sit down,' he said, so I sat.

He leaned forward across his desk, hands clasped, and trained his beady eyes on me.

'It seems you're unclear on your role here. Let me clarify for you. Your job is to get the last drop of blood out of each and every one of the employees in this business. Got it?'

Meeting over.

True story. As bizarre as it sounds, I wish all people who had decided to serve themselves, rather than the people they lead, were like this man. Why?

Because it would make such people who *haven't* chosen people leadership very easy to spot. His lack of care for others was so blatant. His lack of people leadership so easily identifiable. Ultimately, it made it easy for me to decide to leave that CEO and his organisation.

Management and leadership are not synonymous, though you are forgiven for thinking they are – they are often used interchangeably. Sadly, I expect many of you have had a 'manager' who is ostensibly responsible for other people but who couldn't lead hungry teenagers to McDonald's. It's a very demoralising experience.

THE 'L' WORD

Let's have a closer look at this 'L' word: *Leadership*. It's everywhere these days. Thought leadership. Global leadership. Brand leadership. Project leadership. The list goes on. And on. What we'll be talking about specifically in this book is *people* leadership. As an emerging people leader, someone who is leading people for the first time, it's vital that you have a thorough understanding of what leading people actually means for you and for those you lead, so you can make an informed choice about whether you wish to become a people leader, or not.

'But hang on a minute ...', I hear you say, '... I'm already in a leadership *role*, I've already made that decision!' And boom! Sirens go off, lights start flashing, and you've fallen headlong into the first trap.

People leadership is *not* a role. It's a *choice*.

I admit it's pretty mean of me to booby trap the beginning of the book. Let me share with you why I did. My opening story illustrated the perils of being in a leadership role when you haven't chosen to lead the people who are in your care. You may currently be in a role with the words 'manager' or 'leader' tacked on the end and your position description may list the number of direct reports you have, and it may all sound very impressive, but that does not make you a leader.

I'll wager that as you stepped into your first leadership 'role' you may have been bombarded with a selection of new tasks. They might have included:

- approving timesheets
- creating rosters

- approving leave
- filling in a workplace health and safety report if someone had an accident at work
- ensuring your team members are not bullying each other
- running performance 'appraisals'
- hiring people
- letting people go
- and everything in between.

And each of those are important tasks that you will need to get under your belt. These are important *management* tasks. (*Woah there, don't gallop on, just go back and read that again – 'management tasks', that's it – thank you. Okay, please proceed.*) And getting these management tasks correct is essential, isn't it? Your team needs to get paid; they need to take leave, and you need people doing the right jobs in the right place at the right time. But (and it's a b-i-g but), getting those things right *doesn't* make you a great leader. If only it were that easy …

Have you ever heard either of these conversations?

'What was the best thing about your day today, honey?'

'Well, you're not going to believe this, but … they paid me correctly today, isn't that *amazing*?'

Or:

'How was your day?'

'Oh, it was sooo cool, I turned up at the job site and do you know what? The whole team was there! Yeah! Everyone we needed actually turned up and we had the right gear and we could just get on with it straight away!'

'Oh, my goodness, you must be so happy.'

'I am!'

Nup? They don't ring a bell? For me either. Getting the *management* tasks correct stops people from having a bad day, but it doesn't help them have a great day.

'So, what exactly does make the difference?' I hear you say. (*Thank you so much for asking!*)

THAT, my friend, brings us back to leadership.

Trying to get your head around people leadership can be a bit of a challenge – even more challenging than scrambling your way out of that first 'leadership-is-a-choice-and-it's-not-management' booby trap. To be honest, my own people leadership journey reminds me a bit of the midnight-blue coloured gin I was given for Christmas. You *think* you know exactly what you're getting, but the moment you taste it you realise it's something entirely different! And maybe it's the same for you. (*For you fellow gin drinkers, let the record state that the gin turned pink when I added the tonic and it tastes of lavender. Very unusual and highly recommended – but doesn't taste like traditional gin at all!*)

WHERE ARE WE GOING?

As I mentioned, in this book we're talking very specifically about *people* leadership. Not thought leadership, not strategic leadership, just this beautiful, yet complex thing called people leadership.

Let me share what can happen when you focus on people leadership. I'm going to tell you about my daughter Neve's very first day at work. As I write, Neve is 16 years old and she's been working at a local cafe called The Lott as part of their team of waitstaff for about a year. The Lott is owned and led by Steve, and Steve has become Neve's very first leader.

The Lott is the place to be in our town. The cafe opens from 7 am and runs through until 3 pm each afternoon, operating seven days, with an enthusiastic roster of staff in the kitchen and on the floor to keep the place humming.

Neve's first day involved a lot of learning – shadowing Steve and other team members to see how things worked and how to do the basics; how to iron her apron, how to hold the plates, how to deliver coffee without spilling it, what's on the menu, how to clean tables, how to deal with customers, ending up with how to clean the toilets.

At the end of her first shift Steve had organised a team meeting with the whole crew. When I picked Neve up after the meeting she was beaming.

'How was your first day?' I asked.

'It was *amazing*, Mum,' she said. 'It just feels like a little family there. Everyone is friendly and was helping me …', and then she proceeded to tell me all about the ins and outs of her first day.

Day one and she's already feeling part of the 'little family' that is her new work team. *Now that's impressive*, I thought to myself. Impressive, but not surprising if you've ever met Steve.

Steve has a long list of leadership attributes:

- He's genuinely interested in connecting with people; he builds rapport easily and deeply.
- He's an excellent communicator; he asks lots of questions to understand, and shares what he's thinking and working on and what he expects from his team.
- He can focus his team on what's important; not just customer service but excellent hospitality.
- He enjoys developing people; he loves taking on school kids and teaching them the ropes, offering awesome on-the-job mentoring.
- He supports his staff to resolve any problems they're facing, using bucketloads of curiosity and empathy.

And not only that. Steve is also curious, listens deeply and asks great questions. He's not a coach, but he could be. And a great one. And he's always learning. Before he ran the cafe, he was an … acupuncturist! There's a learning curve, right there.

By harnessing and leveraging these leadership attributes Steve has created a positive culture where his team has fun with each other at work and where after only one day, Neve felt part of a little family. That is people leadership in action. It's wonderful for all involved, and for the business.

My dream is that everyone could have a leader like Steve, who makes them feel like a deeply valued member of the team, part of the family, every single day, from day one. A leader who enables every team member to flourish; to become their very best.

How could this happen? How could everyone have a leader like this? How could people *become* leaders like this? Let's face it, as much as we would like to be able to wave our magic wands and control all of those around us, we can only control ourselves. Knowing that, the very best place to start is with YOU!

My wishes for you

If I could have three wishes, this is what I would wish for you:

1. I wish you to become the enabling leader I know you can be.
2. I wish you to become the inspiring leader your team deserves.
3. I wish to see your leadership come into bud, form and bloom, so that you can experience the joy of watching your team flourish under your care.

How are we going to get there? How am I going to make my wishes for you come true? Just as the title suggests, I'm going to help you get on your marks, get set and lead! To do this I'm going to guide you through my framework.

Firstly, I'm going to help you 'get on your marks' by looking at how you're going to learn how to learn. That's a bit of a mouthful, isn't it? How you learn is going to have a huge bearing on how successful you will be, not just as a leader but generally in your life. Together, we'll cover what learning tools you currently have in your metaphorical kit bag and some new ones you can implement. We'll also look at your support crew – all the different people around you who can support you to learn and grow. By the end of this part, you'll feel confident that you have the right mindset, tools and support in place to transition successfully to leading people.

Secondly, you're going to learn about the 'being' of leadership before we even tackle what you're going to be doing. (Get set ...) I'll introduce you to coaching and how you might bring a coaching approach to your leadership. This might be one of the most significant differences you notice as you transition from your previous role to leading people – moving away from advice giving and towards asking questions to help your team come up with their own answers to the challenges they face.

Our third and final step (Lead!) is to consider what you'll be doing when you lead. I like to call these the five duties of leadership. They are:

- connecting with your team
- communicating with your team

- focusing your team
- developing your team
- resolving problems with your team.

Then we'll wrap up the book by helping you create your very own leadership development plan.

TIME TO CHOOSE

Hopefully, this is all sounding pretty appealing to you, but before we go on, I just want to circle back to the point I made earlier about people leadership being a choice. If you're reading this book, you're likely at a crossroads in your career. Maybe you've arrived at an intersection and one sign says 'People Leadership' and the other says 'Technical Expert'.

Which way will you go?

Let's be clear: *they are both good options.*

If you choose to take the leadership fork it will be a rewarding and challenging path. And every step you take down this path, will move you further and further away from the technical expert path – the paths diverge.

If you choose to take the technical expert path it will also be a rewarding and challenging path. As you proceed you deepen your knowledge in your area or areas of expertise until, lo and behold, you have become the guru! Someone who metaphorically, or literally, writes the books in your knowledge area.

Problems arise when you discover one day that while you thought you were busy developing your technical expertise, you're actually on the leadership path. Chances are your people saw the problem waaaaaay before you did.

Your choice to take the leadership path has to be deliberate. It has to be well considered. You have to be aware of the benefits and the sacrifices that come with this choice and step into it wholeheartedly. You must have a desire to lead. You need to commit. When you commit to your own development as a leader you can roll with punches, recover from setbacks and day by day become a better and better leader. A leader your team will be proud of.

It's vitally important for your team. If you don't *choose* to be their leader, why should they choose to contribute at work each day? If you care for your team, your team will care for you. Your team needs to know you're serious about leading them. When they feel your support and encouragement they will engage and give their best. And they will make your life easier, and you will all have more fun! And your business will be much more likely to succeed.

THREE COMMON DERAILERS TO AVOID

There are three things, however, that can totally derail your attempts to become an inspiring and enabling leader. I hate surprises, so let's make sure you're up to the challenge before you read on.

Derailer #1: I've got this!

It's the phrase most us have uttered seconds before disaster strikes. You know the one …

'All good?'

'Sure thing. **I've got this.**' (Cue explosion, sound of shattering glass and the hapless wails of small children.)

'Yeah, right.' *eye roll*

If you're already thinking 'yeah, I know leadership' before you've even begun, I'd suggest you just place this book back on the shelf and back slowly away. Put. The book. Down. It won't be for you! You're going to get the most out of this book if you are open to learning and confident that you've got a lot to learn. You must be someone who is willing to try and fall and get back up again, and then try again and fall again and get back up again and so on, until you get things right. I hope you make tonnes of mistakes, as with every mistake comes a powerful learning. And the quicker you fall, the quicker you'll learn and the quicker you'll grow as a leader. You will have to harness your humility; it's a powerful partner for growth.

Derailer #2: Lack of desire

Oh, and you've got to want it – desire it. The only people who don't learn and grow are those who don't want to. If you want to become an inspiring people leader who enables your team to flourish you have to want to do the work. As an executive coach with over 1,000 hours of coaching experience I can say that I've only ever met two people who were uncoachable. And it was not that each of them didn't have room for improvement. And it wasn't that they didn't have the capacity to improve. They just simply didn't want to, and weren't open to doing the work required. They thought they had it all covered and they didn't want to change. Thanks for coming. Game over!

I feel this quote, by Brian Herbert, which I have on my wall, sums up this issue of desire to learn quite nicely:

> The capacity to learn is a gift; the ability to learn is a skill;
> the willingness to learn is a choice.

Derailer #3: I'm too busy

I'll never forget a short video I watched by the late Jim Rohn about busyness. It really struck a painful chord with me on the home front, and is also directly applicable to work and to our growth and development as leaders. In a nutshell, Jim said that when someone makes a request of our time and we say 'I'm too busy' in response, what we're *actually* saying is 'I don't choose you'. When we're too busy to do one thing, it's because we're choosing to do another thing instead. Makes sense, doesn't it?

I applied this at home. My cricket-mad son had asked me, 'Mum, could you please come and bowl me a few overs?' My response had been, 'I'd love to Miles but I'm a bit busy right now.' Off he went.

Now let's change that wording around.

'Mum, could you please come and bowl me a few overs?' My response with this alternate wording would have been, 'I'd love to Miles but *I don't choose you.*' OUCH! You'll be relieved to know that I didn't actually say those words (even though, sadly, I'm sure that's the meaning he took away from our conversation), but now they're the only words I can hear when someone says 'I'm too busy':

- When you cancel your one-on-one meeting with your team member because you're 'too busy', your team member hears 'I don't choose you'.
- When you arrive late to your team meeting because you were 'too busy' in another meeting, your team hears 'I don't choose you'.
- When you arrive home late to your loved ones because you were 'too busy' at work, they hear 'I don't choose you'.

And, in a similar vein, when you don't undertake your leadership training and development because you're 'too busy', the message you're sending is, 'I don't choose to develop and grow as a leader'.

I would like to ban the words 'I'm too busy'. Clarity on what matters most is the antidote to busyness, and when you know what's important then you can make time to do *those* things and stop doing the things that aren't important. You can ask yourself, 'If I say yes to this, what am I saying no to?' as a way of self-checking whether you are choosing your highest priorities. And remember, 'not choosing' *is* choosing to keep doing what you're doing now. (*That one stings a bit, doesn't it?*)

By picking up this book and turning your mind to your learning and growth as a leader, you are choosing *very* wisely. You are choosing you. Well done. I'm looking forward to being your guide as you navigate this next chapter (*pardon the pun!*) of your development.

WHO AM I TO BE YOUR GUIDE?

I feel very privileged whenever people feel comfortable to share some of their life story with me. I'm big on disclosure and the vulnerability it demonstrates. I'd like to share an 'abridged version' of my backstory so you can get to know me better, to help us connect. I thought I'd write it like a book synopsis, just for fun. Here goes:

Scottish farm girl, turned Master of Science Uni student meets Australian traveller, marries said traveller and emigrates to Australia. After a career U-turn into human resource management, relocates to a new role with iconic Snowy Hydro. After a not-so-fairy-tale ending to first marriage, meets man-of-her-dreams (#therealprince).

Spends next 13 years developing people – company wide and two little people at home – while undertaking a Graduate Diploma in Human Resource Management and coach development just to keep things interesting. Chasing variety, a leadership development consultancy is born: People Mastery. During the next eight years, student transforms into teacher while learning how to navigate challenges; bushfires, global pandemics, book writing and most daunting of all … life with teenagers!

Nearly 50 years in one paragraph – phew!

Seriously though, I have a Bachelor of Arts in Export Studies and Languages from Edinburgh Napier University, a Master of Science in European Policy, Law & Management from Robert Gordon University and a Grad Diploma from Deakin Uni in HR Management. It's not your typical leadership development consultant pathway, but that's what makes me unique, right? I became a certified professional with the Australian Human Resources Institute in 2011. Then I undertook an International Coach Federation accredited coach training program with IECL, completing levels 1, 2 and 3 and team coaching programs. I was honoured to be awarded Coach of the Year by Lever Transfer of Learning in 2014 and I've completed over 1,000 hours of coaching with clients. I'm an accredited Five Behaviours of a Cohesive Team (Lencioni) Facilitator, DiSC Certified trainer and an MBTI practitioner.

Since founding People Mastery I've partnered with some exceptional Australian and international businesses to support them in their work and enhance my learning at the same time. I've worked with family businesses, corporates, public service and NGOs of all different shapes and sizes, and I love the variety I see across these different organisations. I also notice many commonalities.

I have the privilege of working with different types of leaders in different situations. In the classroom when I'm facilitating emerging leader development programs; in the boardroom when I work with board and executive leadership teams on the dynamics of their leadership; and even quietly, one on one, inside my coaching sessions with young and 'young at heart' leaders who are striving to be the best leaders they can be. I see and hear their troubles and challenges, their wins and opportunities, and I always feel honoured to be of support to them as they develop.

And I've been a leader too. I've always had a burning desire to lead a team, and as I developed through my career I had the opportunity to lead small teams inside some of the organisations I worked in. Deep down though, the drive to have my very own team unconstrained by the parameters of someone else's 'rules' and someone else's culture formed, and inspired me to start my own business to make that desire a reality. I'm now fortunate to have a fantastic team of six (Ash, Bec, JD, Jen, Kirsty and Kristi) and I take my duty to take care of and lead my team very seriously. You'll hear more about these fabulous ladies throughout the book.

I'm far from perfect. I don't get it right all the time when it comes to leadership. Who does? My intention though is always to inspire my team and enable them to flourish. I'm looking forward to sharing my knowledge, skills and experience with you and providing you with a useful framework and specific actions to help you move onwards and upwards.

Right. I think that's more than enough about me. I wrote this book for you, so let me explain how you can use it to become the inspiring and enabling leader I know you can be.

HOW TO USE THIS BOOK

This book is set out in three parts. I'd recommend that you work through them in sequence; part I, then part II, then part III. They are designed to build on each other, and you'll find that part II – which is all about developing your coaching approach to leadership – serves as both the foundation and the vessel in which all the duties of leadership (in part III) can successfully occur. Once you've digested and applied part II it will become so much easier to implement the five duties of leadership.

Each chapter begins with a quote. I love quotes, and as you'll know you often see quotes in books, but mine are a bit different. They're not random picks from ancient gurus and the like, they're carefully selected from authors and thought leaders I admire and whose work I've studied. Connected to the quotes is the reading list. Some books I specifically mention in the text, others are included as additional reading to further develop your depth of leadership knowledge. All are included in the 'Recommended Reading' list at the end of the book. Enjoy them all.

Take. Your. Time. Gobbling up the book in one sitting and proclaiming 'I'm done!' is not going to serve you very well. (I do hope you find it full of tasty morsels though!) I'd suggest that you read each chapter and then pause. Let each chapter run around in your mind for a while. Reflect on what you read. What did you discover? What are your reflections on that discovery? And what action are you going to take to implement your learning? At the end of each chapter, you'll find a one-page learning reflection. These set out the key discoveries in each chapter, some questions for you to reflect on. If you really want to power up your learning, answer them all thoroughly. Finally, the summary contains some simple actions (they're habits, and we'll talk more about that later) that you might like to experiment with to apply your leadership learnings in your everyday work.

In some chapters you may find that you're on top of things – excellent! If that's the case, look for the 'fine tunes' or tweaks you can make to become even better in that area than you already are. There's nothing like a timely refresher to buff up your leadership and give it that extra sparkle! Some chapters may have content for you that feels brand new – super! Take extra time in these chapters to glean all the learnings you can and get the best possible value from the book.

All the examples in this book are real. Some from my direct experience, some shared experiences from my family and friends, colleagues and clients. I like to celebrate the positive examples – my shining stars – so real names are used where that person has given their kind permission. I've set out their full names in the appreciation pages at the back of the book. I also use some examples from what my husband calls 'The Book of What Not to Do'; understandably in those examples, where people have shared their learnings and/or would like to preserve their anonymity I've changed the names and marked them with an *.

Once you've been through the book once, keep dipping back into it to make sure you stay on track. Need to brush up on your listening? Dip back into the chapter on listening. Team getting a little bit distracted and need some refocusing? Hop back into the 'Focusing your team' chapter. Every time you invest effort into implementing your learnings through adjusting your leadership habits you and your team will be the beneficiaries.

ARE YOU READY TO GO?

You've made it to the end of the introduction. Yay! That's a good start! How are you feeling? Are you excited about enhancing your learning? Ready to jump in boots and all to developing your coaching approach? Excited about fulfilling your leadership duties? Wooo-hoooo! It sounds like people leadership is right up your alley!

I believe that you can become an inspiring and enabling leader, and you sound like you're up for the journey. So, what are you waiting for? Put your training shoes on, get on your marks, get set and let's go!

Enjoy the ride!

Anna

'Between stimulus and response there is a space. In that space is our power to choose our response. In our response lies our growth and our freedom.'

Viktor Frankl

Part I

ON YOUR MARKS

On the cover of this book you might have noticed the traffic lights. This first part of the book is symbolised by the red light. A stop light; a pause, or a space, for preparation before you get set (amber) and lead (green). We've all heard the overused clichés around planning: failing to plan is planning to fail, yada-yada-yada – but as you embark on your development as a leader it's vital that you pause and reflect on where you are now and how you're going to navigate this next phase of your career.

With that in mind, let's perform a reality check to see where you're at. We're going to have a look at:

- *Self:* that's you!
- *Systems:* the ones you're working in, inside your organisation.
- *Support crew:* the people around you who you can draw on for support.

But before that, let's help you get the most out of this book by supporting you in learning how to learn.

'If knowledge is power, knowing what we don't know is wisdom.'

Adam Grant

1

LEARNING HOW TO LEARN

Before you learn how to lead, you need to *learn how to learn*. Of course, I appreciate that you went to school and you learnt there (or maybe not so much). And then perhaps you went to uni or college or tech and you learnt there too. The big difference between learning inside those institutions and learning inside organisations is who's directing the learning. Predominantly in educational institutions it's the teachers and lecturers. If you want to learn inside an organisation, it's *you*. You may be fortunate to work in a business that has a strong development focus with a smorgasbord of development options for you to choose from. If so, count your blessings. On the other hand, you may work somewhere that the responses to your questions about personal development sound remarkably like the chirping of crickets. If that is your situation, don't despair: the first thing I'm going to do is guide you through some effective and simple learning tools that will set you up for success as you learn how to lead.

In this chapter we're going to look at one model (the stages of learning), three tools for learning (reading, reflection and journalling) and one tool for learning application (habit formulation). If you already have some of these tools in your kit bag – awesome! This will be a useful refresher. If not – even more awesome – you're going to learn a lot in these first few pages.

Rightio … let's kick off with the learning model.

THE FOUR STAGES OF LEARNING MODEL

As Adam says, 'knowing what we don't know is wisdom', and this stage of 'knowing what you don't know' is just one of four levels within the learning model I'm going to share with you. At every step along your leadership development journey, I'd encourage you to refer back to this model – ask yourself, which stage am I in? And how do I move forward from here? I'm sure you're going to discover that at various times you are at different stages in the different components that make up people leadership. Let's have a look at a learning model – which sets out these different levels – now.

Noel Burch of Gordon Training International developed the Conscious Competence model in the 1970s. It's an oldie but a goodie. It identifies how consciousness and skill level change as we learn something new. Learning to drive provides an excellent example of how this learning model applies in real life.

Conscious Competence model

At level one, we are unconsciously unskilled and we don't know what we don't know, or that we need to learn something. It's a blind spot. In our driving example, this would be a soon-to-be L-plater who doesn't even know that a 'hill start' is a thing.

When we move to level two, we become conscious of our incompetence; we know what we don't know. It's an opportunity. When our L-plater gets in the car for the first time and is unable to perform a hill start – where she has to balance the clutch, the accelerator and the handbrake without rolling backwards – she now knows what she doesn't know.

As we move to level three – conscious competence – we now know what to do and can do it. It's become a skill. Our L-plater's skills have developed, and now when she gives the hill start her full attention she can pull away smoothly.

Finally – at level four – we become unconsciously competent. This means we can perform the skill almost automatically. (This can also be a hidden talent; we'll talk more about that later.) For now, back to our driver. She can now regularly perform hill starts whenever needed and doesn't have to focus on it much anymore. She can successfully execute the hill start seemingly effortlessly.

You can see the driving analogy demonstrates how an L-plater progresses through the four levels to achieve unconscious competence. Back to you now. As you're reading this book, I'm sure you're going to experience the four different levels, even if you don't roll through them in order.

It might look like this. As you're reading this book …

You finish a chapter and think, *Oh my gosh, I'd never even thought of that as related to people leadership*. You've just discovered an area where prior to your reading you were unconsciously incompetent.

Or …

Now that you've had that discovery, you reflect, *Geez, I really don't think I'm very good at that yet*, and you've moved into conscious incompetence.

Or …

You made your discovery and reflect, *That's cool. When I think about that I can do it quite well. I just need to keep doing more of that to improve*, and you're in conscious competence.

Or …

When you reflect on feedback you've had from people over the years, they've always mentioned that you're very skilled at resolving conflict. You don't really need to think about it, you just seem to navigate it smoothly and effectively. Unconscious competence. You can just do it without thinking.

At this stage in the book, we're applying the learning model to you. I'm sure you can already see how useful the learning model will also be with your team. When you're trying to figure out where they are on their development journey you can revisit this model.

Don't worry if you suspect you're a bit all over the place in terms of people leadership. That's perfectly normal. Some things you'll already be smashing out of the park (unconsciously competent), and some things you won't even have realised were in the park (unconscious incompetence). That's what this book is all about – helping you move through the levels towards level four: leading with ease.

Now that we've got that model under our belts, let's move on to our first learning tool. The good news is you're already using it (woo-hoo!): reading.

READING

Did you know that reading can be one of the most powerful ways to learn and grow? Barack Obama says, 'Reading is a gateway skill that makes all other learning possible.' I love that. Reading enables you to access some of the most brilliant wisdom in the world from the comfort of your own lounge, or now with audiobooks even in your car or on your bike! Whether you read or listen to books, articles, blog posts or newsletters, when you are consuming quality content you are learning and growing. I must confess that I love books, though at different stages in my life it has been difficult to make reading a priority. At one point I joined a book club to hold myself accountable for making reading a priority – it worked! Now I run leadership book clubs inside organisations as a way of building knowledge, and at the same time creating a supportive peer group.

Interestingly, feedback from my book group participants who tried both listening to the book and reading the book found that reading the book helped the content land more effectively. When you're actually reading you can make notes in the margins, highlight different passages and quotes that stand out to you and even note down questions that might arise. While writing on your books may sound sacrilegious – *it may bring back memories of scribbling on books as a child and being reprimanded!* – it's an extremely useful practice as an adult as a way of highlighting pertinent aspects in the books we read. Or you could consider using sticky labels to bring your attention to certain pages if you just can't bring yourself to write in the book.

If you find a great book and take lots of learnings from it, recommend it to others in your workplace. You could also set up your own people leadership book club – maybe you could start with this book?! – and have a great discussion about what landed and what didn't, and what you're going to implement into your own people leadership practice.

And if for some reason you find reading a bit too challenging or time consuming, you might consider subscribing to a book summary site, or accessing free book summary sites, where you can glean the key learnings in bite-sized chunks rather than having to consume the whole book.

REFLECTION

Reflection is giving serious thought and consideration to how you are leading. It's when you take a step back or a step up and observe *how you are being* and *what you are doing.* You know when you see yourself in a dream, as if you're watching yourself in a movie? This is the position you are taking during reflection. It takes time and conscious effort to undertake reflection. When you're rushing through work and life it is very hard to step back quietly into reflection. Let's look at some practical ways to engage in reflection, so you can do so more easily.

You can do it on your own (self-guided reflection) or you can do it with another person. You might engage one of your support crew (which we'll cover in chapter 4): a trusted colleague or confidante perhaps to whom you can speak your thoughts and regard them afresh, or even a professional coach.

In this section we'll cover two tools to support you with self-guided reflection. That way you can get started immediately. These tools are:

- the Discovery Reflection Action (DRA) cycle
- journalling.

The DRA Cycle

Let me take you on a wee journey. (*Oh! Remember I'm Scottish? Well, to be honest I'm a dual citizen: Scottish/Australian. So, you might find a few 'wees' sneaking into the book. It's Scottish for 'little' or 'small'.*)

Take a moment. Sit back comfortably and take a deep breath in. And now slowly exhale, relax, and then imagine this: you're out for a walk and you come across a pristine lake. There's not a breath of wind, it's a gloriously sunny day, with not a cloud in the sky. The surface of the lake is as smooth as glass, and as you stand there looking out over the lake you see your reflection looking back at you. As you consider your mirror image, you see yourself from a slightly different perspective. Maybe you look relaxed, maybe a little tense. Or perhaps you see everything in order, or one or two minor things out of place and you make a few adjustments – you roll down your sleeves and tie up your shoelaces, and you run your fingers through your hair, and before you know it, you're back to rights again. Satisfied, you continue on your walk alongside the lake.

Using the analogy above I want to help you see how you can bring the cycle of reflection, which is usually invisible to the eye, to your development as a leader. When in reflection you enable yourself to take a figurative step back and regard yourself anew – what are you *discovering* about yourself? Just notice, without judgment.

Sleeves are up, shoelaces are undone, hair's a bit messy.

Then you move into the *reflection* stage – given I notice these things, what do I think about that?

I'm feeling cold, I may trip over if I don't tie my laces, my hair's getting in my eyes.

And then finally to the *action* stage – given my reflections about my discoveries, what, if any, action do I want to take?

I need to roll my sleeves down; I need to tie my laces; and I need to move my hair out of the way.

This is your introduction to a reflective cycle known as DRA – Discovery, Reflection and Action. We'll be using this cycle throughout the book to highlight key learnings, elicit your reflections on those discoveries and then invite you to put in place some key actions to move you forward. You'll notice that I've purposely included this tool in the chapter summaries, to help you become familiar with it. We'll also examine it in detail in chapter 12.

Discovery Reflection Action cycle

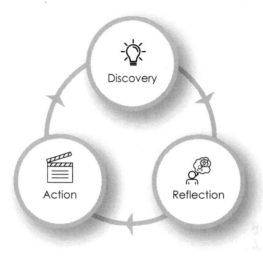

D: What are your new discoveries?

R: When you reflect on your discoveries, what have you learned?

A: Based on your discoveries and reflections, what action could you take now to further improve?

Here's a real example of another self-guided reflective practice that a coaching client of mine had. You will see how she linked some planning with an effective DRA cycle.

Anne* was at the time a people leader in one of Australia's largest telecommunications companies. She had a neat little weekly reflective practice. On a Monday she thought about her week ahead and asked herself which three conversations were going to be the most important this week. Then she considered what she'd like to get out of those conversations, how exactly she would like them to go, and then she planned accordingly. Then at the end of the week she would reflect on how they went, taking some time on a Friday to sit back and consider what actually happened. This would lead her to review what went well and what she might do differently, which would enable her to get an even better result the next time. Then she would implement those actions the following week. I loved how Anne kept her reflection tight – focusing on three conversations – not attempting to change ALL her conversations at once. Starting small and building up her abilities over time would ultimately shape all her conversations, but she started with something really achievable to begin with.

Leadership tip: the dancefloor and the balcony

A slightly different way of gaining a different perspective through reflection is to use one of my favourite analogies: the dancefloor and the balcony. Often when we're leading, we are actually 'on the dancefloor'. We are *doing* leadership; demonstrating leadership behaviours like connecting and communicating with our people, focusing them on priorities and so on. If we're not careful, that can end up being all we do. It is important from time to time to step up on to the balcony (*or the mezzanine level in that cool leadership nightclub of yours*) and have a good look down at what is happening on the dancefloor. Maybe you're doing a fine impression of John Travolta's Saturday Night Fever while everyone else is doing Gangnam style! Ooops! Getting up on the balcony is another way of reflecting on what is going on and what you might need to do differently to get a better result with your leadership. You might like to consider booking some 'balcony time' into your diary.

JOURNALLING

Following on from reflection, journalling is reflective writing. This is just a neat way of saying 'writing stuff down as a way of clarifying and distilling your thinking', and if you have a stationery fetish it's a great excuse to buy a nice new journal from your favourite store!

This beautiful line by Dawson Trotman captures the value of journalling:

> Thoughts disentangle themselves when they pass through the lips and fingertips.

Capturing your thoughts in writing (through your fingertips) helps you make sense of what you're thinking and feeling, and consider them anew. It's interesting how much clarity you can get by writing something down. You read what you've written on the page and then – BING! – the light bulb switches on and you have a different insight about that thing. In my experience, writing a book feels much like writing a really, really, really long journal. I find that as I write things down, I have increasing clarity about my thoughts and there's a whole heap of disentanglement going on.

Are you wondering whether you should type or handwrite your journal? There's some interesting research indicating that if you're keen to be more mindful, explore your emotions, generate new ideas and insights then handwriting will serve you best. If you simply want to keep a record of information then you can stick with typing. Given that journalling is intended to be a reflective, developmental process my recommendation would be to handwrite your notes. These days of course handwritten journals can be digital; you can handwrite your journal with a stylus on your favourite tablet or iPad or you might consider using a reMarkable like me.

Whichever medium you choose, don't worry, I'm not encouraging you to write a book! (*Not just yet, anyway.*) I would, though, strongly encourage you to simply begin. Just start really small. You could use a little phrase to stimulate your writing – maybe one of these will be helpful:

- What went well today was …
- The one thing I learned today was …
- Three things I'm grateful for are …
- What I'm learning about people leadership is …
- When I stand on the balcony, what I notice is …
- One thing I could do differently is …

Or create a little phrase of your own.

Run a little experiment with yourself. Pick a timeframe to experiment with journalling. Maybe you set yourself a goal of writing for 10 minutes once a day, or half an hour a week, or a paragraph a day (whatever feels achievable for you), and then stick to that for at least a month. When you get to the end of that period, what do you notice? If it's useful – awesome! If not – no problem, you can just try something else.

Time for a quick recap. We are now one model and three learning tools down, with one learning application tool to go.

Are you still with me? Excellent. Time to get our habits on.

HELPFUL HABITS

Learning without application is like a joke without a punchline. It's vital you transfer your learning to your work so that you can improve. Why else would you bother?

When I first joined Snowy Hydro in 2001, I received a call at my desk one day from a person who was about to attend a leadership program we were running ...

> 'Is this going to be one of those programs where we attend and then go back to our work and just keep doing the same things we were doing before?'
>
> 'No. This will NOT be one of those programs,' I replied incredulously.

While I was dumbfounded at the time, I look back now and appreciate the candour. How many programs are actually like that in organisations? Too many! I want to prevent you from falling into that trap. I want to help you transfer your learnings to your work as a people leader so you can perpetually improve. Habits are the key.

Applying your learning through habits

There are many excellent books on habits (I've put a list together for you later in the book). One author in particular who has written about habits and whose work I adore is Michael Bungay Stanier (affectionately known as MBS), who has written among other books *The Coaching Habit: Say less, ask more and change the way you lead forever*. In his book, MBS sets out a habit formula as follows:

When X happens, instead of doing Y, I will do Z.

Where X is the triggering event, Y is the behaviour you are going to stop doing and Z is the behaviour you're going to start doing.

Here are a few examples to put the formula in context:

- When a team member arrives late for work at the cafe (triggering event), instead of letting that go (stop doing), I will take them aside and ask them if they're okay and ask about why they were late and make sure they are clear on our expectations of punctuality (start doing).
- When I've finished my tasks for the day on the job site (triggering event), instead of just closing the site and heading home (stop doing), I will think about three good things I've seen the team do that day and share that feedback with team members before they leave (start doing).
- When I'm struggling to lead a tricky team member (triggering event), instead of going round and round in circles in my own head (stop doing), I will reach out to my leader for guidance (start doing).

Leading people is all about who you are being and how you are behaving (aka what you're doing), and as habits are recurring behaviour loops, looking at how we might change our habits is an incredibly effective way of changing and improving our behaviours. It sounds so simple, doesn't it? And the formula IS simple, but that doesn't mean changing habits is easy.

If you've ever tried to modify your eating habits, you'll know just what I mean here:

When I'm feeling hungry in the afternoon (triggering event), instead of eating cake (stop doing), I'll have a large glass of water and a piece of fruit (start doing).

Simple? Yes. Easy? Hell no! Changing your leadership habits is going to be soooo much easier than that one!

You've *almost* made it to the end of the first chapter. Nice. I'd like you to think of this first chapter as the first of two bookends. This chapter on learning to learn is the first bookend, then you're going to have mountains of rich content on learning to lead in the middle, and then at the end of the book you'll find a short chapter on creating your very own people leadership development plan; bookend number two.

You'll find that I've distilled the key elements of each chapter into a neat summary for you at the end of the chapter. You can use the cycle of Discovery, Reflection, Action in each chapter summary to identify and capture your development gaps as you read. Let's briefly run through what a development gap might look like:

- It might be a **behavioural** gap. You'd like to be more courageous and step into the feedback for improvement conversations you need to have with your team members, but instead you've been avoiding them.
- Or it might be a **skills** gap. You want to support your team members to create a development plan, but you don't know what a good plan looks like, or how to go about it.
- Or it might be a **knowledge** gap. There's a new organisational priority for your team that you need to get everyone across, but at this stage you're not even sure what it's all about!
- More than likely, it will be an interesting combination of all of the above.

Take your time to work through the DRA at the end of each chapter. Experiment with one of the suggested habits, or create one of your own. I'll help you draw all the gaps together when you get to the final chapter to create your very own people leadership development plan.

DRA learning reflection

Discoveries:

- [ ] Reading is a powerful way to learn and grow.
- [ ] Reflection enables us to see ourselves, others and situations from a different perspective.
- [ ] Coaching is facilitated and supported reflection.
- [ ] Moving from the dancefloor to the balcony enables us to reflect more broadly.
- [ ] Journalling, like other forms of reflection, creates clarity.
- [ ] When you want to develop you need to be clear on your development gaps.
- [ ] Developing new habits helps us adjust our behaviour and bridge development gaps.

Reflection questions:

- [ ] How regularly do you undertake self-development activity? Daily? Weekly? Monthly? Quarterly? Rarely?
- [ ] What do you think might be a sustainable frequency for you?
- [ ] Which reflection option would work best for you?

Actions to choose from:

☐ When I have my lunch break, instead of checking social media, I will read five pages of a book relevant to my development.

☐ When I'm organising my week, instead of jamming my diary full of back-to-back appointments, I will book in three reflection appointments so I can get on the balcony and have a good look around.

☐ When I identify my development gaps, instead of just writing them on a list and forgetting about them, I will select the most important one and create a supportive habit to implement.

'In a growth mindset, challenges are exciting rather than threatening. So rather than thinking, oh, I'm going to reveal my weaknesses, you say, wow, here's a chance to grow.'

Carol Dweck

Chapter 2

LEARNING ABOUT YOURSELF

How well do you know yourself? I'm not talking '168 cm, silver hair, brown eyes and I like cake' kind of knowing (which might be true but is useless); I'm talking deep knowing. The kind of self-knowledge which allows you to stand assuredly in who you are and what you offer to the world. And in the case of people leadership, knowledge of your internal resources on which you can draw as you learn how to lead.

This might sound a bit daunting if you haven't reflected on these things before; no matter, I'm going to gently guide you through an initial exploration of the things that make you, you! In this chapter you're going reflect on your beliefs about people, your personal values, and your skills and talents and how they will influence and inform how you lead people.

To begin this chapter we're going to jump inside your head and look at your mindset.

WHICH MINDSET DO YOU HAVE?

How do you know which mindset you have? Before I have a chance to influence your responses, have a look at the following statements and decide which ones you most agree with. Be honest, now!

1. People have a certain amount of intelligence, and there isn't any way to change it.
2. No matter who you are, there isn't much you can do to improve your basic abilities and personality.
3. People are capable of changing who they are.
4. You can learn new things and improve your intelligence.
5. People either have particular talents, or they don't. You can't just acquire talent for things like music, writing, art or athletics.
6. Studying, working hard, and practising new skills are all ways to develop new talents and abilities.

If you tend to agree with statements 1, 2, and 5, you probably have a more fixed mindset. If you agree with statements 3, and 4, 6, you probably tend to have a growth mindset.

If you haven't heard of fixed or growth mindsets before, you're about to learn about a really interesting concept. For the rest of you this will be a timely refresher. The research into fixed and growth mindsets was carried out by Carol Dweck and captured in her book *Mindset: Changing the way you think to fulfil your potential*, which was published in 2006.

In a nutshell, mindsets relate to whether you believe your intelligence and talent are fixed or changeable traits. With a fixed mindset you believe that you've got what you've got; you have a certain amount of intelligence and talent and that's never going to change. If you believe in the phrase 'you can't teach an old dog new tricks' that's a warning bell that you're sitting in the fixed mindset.

With a growth mindset you believe that these traits can be improved upon with commitment and hard work. Basically, you believe that you can grow your own mind – now that's cool!

Back now to your responses to the questions. If you landed with the growth mindset statements – great! And if you landed with the fixed mindset statements – great! Now you know where you're at. Now you get to choose which mindset you'd like to move forward with. No matter where you've landed right now, we can all improve and strengthen our ability to harness a growth mindset.

If any of you were thinking, 'Oh dear, those poor people with the fixed mindsets, they're done for!'... *you're* revealing a fixed mindset about people with fixed mindsets – it's a trap, right?

Think about how this plays out in your workplace. You have a team member who's struggling for some reason – maybe you know why, maybe you don't (yet). If you take a fixed mindset to this, you'll be thinking things like 'they'll never change', or, 'there's no point spending any time with them because they're never going to be able to do *that thing*'. But if you take a growth mindset approach to this you'll be thinking, 'I wonder what we could do to help this person improve?', or, 'What am I missing here?', or, 'What could I do differently that would enable this person to behave differently?' How different will that feel to the person concerned? Rather than being treated as a 'write off', they'll be treated with compassion and support and a good dose of curiosity. I wonder what might be possible if we all took that approach?

While I didn't learn about mindsets until I was in my 30s when I came across Carol's work – I am confident that most of the time I'm sitting in a growth mindset. I confess I have my lapses now and again, but now that I know this concept it's easier for me to dust myself off and get back into growth mindset when I slip up. Here's a story from my early career that demonstrates no matter how 'smart' you are, you can always choose a growth mindset:

When I worked as the People & Culture Manager at Snowy Hydro, I had lots of interesting conversations with the executive team, who were a really interesting group of people with extremely diverse knowledge and experience. I remember sitting at my desk one day when one of the executives rang for some advice.

'Anna, I was wondering if you would come and meet with my team and have some development conversations with them one on one, to see what they're thinking and how they might like to develop into the future?'

'I'm happy to help,' I said, 'though I think your team would really appreciate if you would have those conversations with them, rather than me. What do you think?'

'Oh, yes. Actually, I've already had those conversations with them, I just wanted to make sure that I was doing it right.'

How refreshing! This executive was super smart – PhD smart and people smart – AND really humble and still looking for his learning. I'll never forget that conversation; for me it epitomises a growth mindset.

Developing your growth mindset

Here are two things you can do to develop your growth mindset:

- Remind yourself that effort will grow your abilities. The more effort you put in to something, the better you will become at it. The more effort you put in to your development as a leader, the more likely you will become an inspiring people leader. When you're learning, just tell yourself that you haven't got this – *yet*.
- Change the way you perceive 'failure'. A really useful phrase you can use when you hit a speed bump and something doesn't go as you'd planned is to say, 'That's not like me. Next time I will ... [add in what you want to happen the next time].' Nelson Mandela said, 'I never lose. I either win or learn.' Again, that phrase epitomises taking a growth mindset.

Now that you've got your growth mindset switched on, let's look at what else is floating around in your mind. What about your beliefs about people? Have you ever considered what your beliefs are and how they might shape how you lead?

WHAT ARE YOUR BELIEFS ABOUT PEOPLE?

Whenever I run one of our two-day workshops called 'Engaging People' with emerging leaders, we have a very interesting session about participants' beliefs about people. Voicing our beliefs provides us with the opportunity to review and challenge the extent to which they are serving us and the people we lead. I have to confess that the very first time I ran this session I was very daunted by it. I had no idea what people were going to say, and I was worried that the question 'What beliefs do you hold about people?' was going to create a stony silence. I think this was because having tried to answer the question myself prior to the session I realised that it's fairly deep and requires some vulnerability.

The belief cycle

Beliefs are fascinating things, and they run in an internal cycle in our mind – like this:

You can think of it like this:

Our beliefs shape our thoughts and feelings. Our thoughts and feelings then shape our behaviours. Then our behaviours shape the results we get. And funnily enough these results in turn reinforce our beliefs, and so the cycle continues and they become more firmly ingrained in our minds.

Here's an example. If you believe that people are generally lazy and try to get away with doing the least amount of work possible then you might feel frustrated and think that your team is trying to avoid doing their work. Consequently, you are fairly abrupt with them (*Such time wasters!*) and you keep hammering them about delivery (*C'mon people! Seriously!*). As a result, the team feel a bit stressed and are finding it hard to focus, and therefore are struggling to get their work done (which you don't really perceive), which means their work is often submitted late and with several mistakes, and you think, *Aha! I knew they were lazy!*, which confirms the belief you held and so the negative cycle continues.

On the flipside, if you believe that people come to work each day intending to do their best work, you might feel excited and interested in what your team is going to achieve today. Consequently, you are curious about what they're doing and ask helpful questions and provide support. As a result, the team feels encouraged by you and engaged in their work and with their colleagues, and they submit high-quality work and a range of new ideas for consideration. This confirms your belief that your team is here to do their best and the positive cycle continues.

Which belief might serve you best as a people leader, do you think?

I'm not for one moment suggesting that you take on the belief above. Beliefs are highly personal, and they come from our experience (real or perceived), and sometimes they serve us well and sometimes they don't. What I *am* saying is that when we're not aware of our internal beliefs about people we are powerless to challenge and change them. When we dig deeper, we may find that there is a negative belief looping around in our mind that is not serving us well, and it may be detracting from the wonderful things you want to do as a leader.

I hold a belief that evolved in my mind from a book I read many years ago. My cousin Neill was staying with me for a few days as he travelled in Australia. Neill is a kind and curious soul. He's into personal development, exploration and growth, and he was reading a book by James Redfield called *The Celestine Prophecy: An adventure*. Generously, on his departure he left the book for me to read. In a nutshell, the book is written as an adventure and uses the story to discuss various psychological and spiritual ideas rooted in multiple ancient Eastern traditions; really, it's like a parable. I thoroughly enjoyed it, and one of the beliefs that formed for me from reading that book was:

> Everyone I meet is going to teach me something. Maybe something to do, or perhaps something NOT to do. So, I'd better pay attention.

As I hold that belief, I feel curious when I meet new people about what their teaching might be and I feel excited about the discovery. Consequently, I am open to new people, ask curious questions and look for my learnings. I gain many insights from the people I meet and the occasional 'what not to do', and this reinforces my belief that everyone I meet is going to teach me something.

When you begin to lead people, it's important to understand what belief cycles might be running under the surface for you, so you can question and challenge them. Are they assumptions or biases? Is there evidence to support this belief? And probably most important of all, do these beliefs serve you and your team well?

The interesting thing about our beliefs is that you have choices. You are in charge of your beliefs and their impacts; they should not be in charge of you. So, when you uncover one of your beliefs, you can challenge it at each of the stages of the belief cycle:

- Is this **belief** helping or hindering me as a leader?
- Are my **thoughts** helpful or unhelpful?
- What would be a more useful **thought**?
- Are my **feelings** comfortable or uncomfortable?
- What would be a more desirable **feeling**?
- What impact is my **behaviour** having?
- How might I need to change this **behaviour**?
- Are these **results** helping or hindering me as a leader?
- Are these **results** serving the people I lead?

Your beliefs shape your behaviour choices. Therefore, it's important to explore your beliefs and determine whether they are serving you, and others, well as you transition into people leadership. And remember, you can change them any time you choose.

Beliefs are not the only thing that shape your behaviour. Your behaviour is also shaped by your values. Our values are shaped over many years, and are influenced by our family, our culture and heritage, our life experiences and more. Behaviours are on the surface – we can see them in our daily interactions with one another – while the values that drive them lie quietly underneath.

Let's have a look at your values now.

WHAT ARE YOUR VALUES?

If you're going to lead with your values then you'll need to be clear on what your values are, right? This is critical when you want to lead in a way that feels true for you – you will feel and appear more genuine, self-aware and transparent. A commonly used term these days is 'authentic'. Authentic leaders use their values as a guide as they lead their people.

We all have our own values mix

Values are an interesting concept. While we may have some values in common with others, in reality we all have our very own values mix. A little cocktail, if you like, of values which mean the most to us.

The question 'what are your values?' can be tough to answer. You may never have been asked that question before, so perhaps this version of the same question might be more helpful: 'what do you value?' It might be friendship, kindness, honesty, connection, creativity – the list goes on, and on, and on ...

I think there are two types of values which are most relevant to you right now as you transition into leading people:

- your core values
- your aspirational values.

Let's have a look at each type.

Core values

Core values by their very nature are the values at your core: the things that are central to who you are. Often, they form part of our own description of who we are. Perhaps you think of yourself as a kind person, or a courageous person, or an honest person. Similarly, when we get to know people, we can start to have insight into their values. When you first meet someone, you don't know what their values are – very few people come with their values tattooed on their arms (some do, though!). But as you get to know them you may start to deduce their values from their behaviours. Behaviours provide a window through which you can see people's values. Likewise, the behaviours *you* choose will give others insight into *your* values.

Perhaps you have a team member who is always looking out for other team members, performing small gestures of support, asking whether their help is needed. They volunteer after hours with a local charity and coordinate a sponsored walking event at work. Maybe one of their core values is service, or perhaps it's kindness, or something else – as we get to know them and see their behaviours, we can start to see the values which are driving their behaviour.

Where do our core values come from? Our core values develop over time, they might come from our parents or family – maybe one of your parents was big on 'respect' and that's something you also hold dear. Or they might come from our schooling – maybe your school had a value of 'excellence' and again this was something that resonated with you. They might also come from your experiences in the world – maybe you've spent some time volunteering and you have a value of 'service'.

While they become fairly stable as we grow older, particular experiences and life events may still adjust your values. You, or someone you may know, may have had a significant health scare – maybe a cancer diagnosis, or a stroke, or a car accident – and it causes a values review. Sometimes we notice a marked change in their behaviour post event as a different value comes to the fore. The person has a new value as their priority and now their behaviours evolve to make sure that they are in tune with that value from that point forward. The person might turn the dial down on work and turn it up on time with their family. They make their family their priority. I call that alignment; your behaviours are in alignment with your values.

Aspirational values

Aspirational values are values that you would like to hold, but you're not consistently demonstrating them through your behaviours – *yet*. As you're thinking about the type of people leader you'd like to become, you may have considered some additional values that you feel are important. Maybe you want to be known as a caring leader, or an honest leader, or a supportive leader, or an inspiring leader, and maybe you feel that you haven't got this quite down pat yet. Maybe you're already on the path to adopting a new value, but your behaviours are a bit patchy at this stage – sometimes you're nailing it, and sometimes, well … not so much! It's all part of your learning curve.

Getting clear on how you might be behaving *when* you are living a certain value will help you put this value into practice. It will help you walk your talk. What can be useful is to consider someone who you think currently lives this value really well. For example, if you wanted to be a more authentic leader – more comfortable in your own skin, more self-assured, more honest in your opinions – who do you know, or know of, that demonstrates this value? Maybe it's your own leader, or a colleague. Or someone famous; say, Malala Yousafzai or Barack Obama. What do you see them doing that tells you they are an authentic leader, someone who demonstrates the value of authenticity? When you identify their behaviours, you can choose to bring them into your own practice.

What if you don't know what your values are?

If you are unclear about what your values are or what you would like them to be, there are a few different things you can do to get more insight.

Option 1: Review your own behaviours

Think about the behaviours you demonstrate every day. Write each one down individually on a sticky note. If you were to cluster them into groups of like behaviours, what would the labels be on each group? Would they be 'generosity' or 'contribution' or 'care' or 'fun'?

Once you're aware of the labels – in other words, your lived values – then you can consider how you feel about these values. Are they the values you would like to be driving your leadership, or would you like to tweak them? Up to you.

Let's just say that you've uncovered an 'unsavoury' value; let's pick 'arrogance' as an example. This presents you with a choice. Which value would you actually like to be demonstrating *instead*, and which behaviours should you be choosing so you can move away from arrogance? You might select 'humility', and start by demonstrating behaviours such as asking for help, admitting when you're wrong and apologising.

Option 2: Review the values and behaviours of your role models

You may also look at others you respect and admire and ask yourself two questions:

- What values do I see them demonstrating through their behaviours?
- Which of those values do I aspire to emulate?

Then select some of these behaviours to implement.

Option 3: Reflect on times when someone stepped on your values

Interestingly, sometimes we're not aware that we hold a particular value dear until someone 'steps' on it. Have you ever had that experience when someone does or says something and it's like a million alarm bells have just gone off in your mind?

> *EMERGENCY, EMERGENCY, WOOP, WOOP, WOOP,*
> *VALUES BREACH!!!*

It's like someone has just stomped on something very important to you and every cell of your being screams out in defence. If, or when, that situation occurs for you, just be curious. You might ask yourself a few questions:

- What is it about this situation that is most concerning for me?
- What is this person doing, or not doing, that doesn't sit well with me?
- What would I rather have happen in this situation, and why?
- Which of my values do I feel is being contravened here?

For me, these alarm bells can go off when something unfair is happening, as I have a strong sense of equity and justice. Taking time to reflect on these situations can help us define which values are important to us and which are not.

Option 4: Ask other people what they think your values are

This is a fascinating and illuminating exercise.

Select a handful of people you trust. People who know you really well. They may be family, friends, your leader, colleagues or team members, and ask them, 'If you were to describe me in three words, what words would you choose?' Once you've gathered their feedback you will likely start to see patterns in their responses. A lovely friend of mine is most often described as 'kind and generous' by others, and her key value is kindness. She behaves in accordance with her values.

When you receive their feedback, you have choices.

If what they're seeing identifies values that you feel are 'just right' for you, that's great. Just keep on going and now perhaps you will feel clearer on what your core values are.

If what they're seeing in some way feels a little jarring, and doesn't feel quite like the values you would like to be demonstrating, you can choose to behave in a different way that would feel better for you. You are now in a position to select an aspirational value – one you would like to be living – and start behaving in accordance with that value. When you choose an aspirational value – let's just say 'service' as an example – then ask yourself, 'If I were to behave in accordance with a value of service, what would people see me doing?' Then start doing those things!

The way I see it, behaviours are like your clothes. Every morning when you wake up you get to choose what you put on. Similarly, you really do get to choose how you behave. Sometimes you may feel your behaviours are a reaction to someone else's behaviours – that's part of being human, isn't it? But when you keep coming back to your values, you will make better behaviour choices and you'll feel a lovely sense of alignment as you lead through your values.

How do you use your values?

When you lead your people through your values, you are using your values to help you make decisions. A-ha! *They are a decision-making tool.* When you come to a metaphorical fork in the road and you're trying to decide, should I go right or left? You can come back to your values and decide which fork your values are indicating. For example, if you have a value of fairness, you would ask yourself, which fork best satisfies my value of fairness – the right one? Okay, let's go right. When you are clear on your values and lead through them, you will feel a strong sense of inner alignment.

Phew! Mindsets, beliefs and values ... they are meaty topics, aren't they? I hope that this last section may be a bit easier for you to get your head around: your skills and talents. Did I just hear a *groan* ... ? C'mon now, I know some of you do find it hard to *talk* about what you're good at, but you're just reading and thinking at this stage. You. Can. Do. This.

WHAT ARE YOUR CURRENT SKILLS AND TALENTS?

You chose to keep reading? Good on you! So, when you're embarking on this journey to becoming a truly exceptional people leader, you need to know your starting position ('On your marks ...', remember?). Otherwise, you won't know in which direction you should head to reach your destination. This again is an exercise in self-reflection. How well do you know your current skills and talents? How well can you answer the following questions?

When it comes to people leadership ...

1. What are your strengths and development opportunities?
2. What motivates you and what stresses you?
3. What are your hidden talents and (trick question) blind spots?
4. What do you find easy?
5. What do you find hard?
6. What brings you joy?
7. How would other people answer these questions about you?
8. How do other people *actually* answer these questions about you?

While questions 7 and 8 may look very similar, they are actually quite different. You can answer question 7 all by yourself – it asks you to stand in the shoes of another person and see yourself through their eyes. It's a powerful exercise in perspective taking. It's actually a classic interview question, and over the years I've heard some hilarious 'accidental' answers. It usually goes something like this:

Me:	'And can you tell me about a time when you had to have a difficult conversation with a team member at work? How did you handle that situation?'
Interviewee:	'Oh well, I remember when [insert textbook interview answer here] ...'
Me:	'Oh, yes? Thank you. And if I asked your current teammates about how that conversation went, what do you think they would say?'
Interviewee:	'Well, they'd probably say that I charged in like a bull in a china shop ... [*followed by that *bunny in the headlights* look combined with the thought ... OMG did I actually just say that out loud ... ??!!*]

Yes, this does actually happen! If you could video these interviews they would make the best blooper reels! Anyway, hopefully you can see my point. Taking turns to 'sit in other people's shoes' and see yourself differently adds to your self-awareness. Write down a list of four or five people who you interact with a lot, and if you can, people who are different to one another in some way – different styles, different experiences, different roles – and consider what they might say about you.

After you've done that, you could move onto question 8 and actually ask them. It will be fascinating to see how your anticipated answers align (or misalign) with what they actually say.

What is the value of being able to see ourselves as others see us? There's a clue in two lines in the final verse of a poem called *To a Louse* by Robbie Burns (famous Scottish Poet) in 1786:

> '... To see ourselves as others see us!
> It would from many a blunder free us ...'

When we can see ourselves as others see us it helps us avoid making mistakes. Especially mistakes that we may have previously been blind to. (You can read the whole poem at the back of the book.)

Once you've answered these questions, you will have a much better insight into where you are now, your current capabilities and the internal resources you can draw upon as you learn to lead.

DRA learning reflection

Discoveries:
- Your mindset is your choice. Choose a growth mindset!
- When you have a growth mindset you believe that you can improve yourself through commitment and hard work.
- Your beliefs about people shape your thoughts, feelings, behaviours and, accordingly, the results you get.
- When your beliefs are unhelpful, you can challenge them and choose to demonstrate different behaviours and achieve a different result.
- Core values are the things you place value on, which drive your behaviour.
- Aspirational values are the things you would like to place value on, which aren't driving your behaviour *yet*.
- Get clear on your values and use them to guide your decisions.
- Understanding your skills and talents enables you to determine where you are now and what capabilities you can draw on as you learn to lead.

Reflection questions:
- On a scale of 1 to 10, with 1 low and 10 high, how consistently are you holding a growth mindset?
- Where, or about what, might you be holding a fixed mindset? What impact is that having?
- What beliefs do you hold about people? How well are they serving you and your people?

- What existing unhelpful beliefs might you challenge?
- What are your core values? How are they showing up in your leadership?
- What, if any, aspirational values do you intend to hold into the future?
- How clear are you on your skills and talents? How often are you using them?

Actions to choose from:
- When I'm struggling with something, instead of thinking 'I can't do this', I will tell myself 'I need to spend more time learning how to do this'.
- When I make decisions, instead of just rushing in, I will use my values to guide my decision making.
- When I'm learning how to lead, instead of randomly trying new things, I will take time to build on my existing skills and talents.

'Human systems give an organisation a structure for tying its operations, culture and management together, even when leaders aren't around to remind people.'

Patrick Lencioni

Chapter 3

THE IMPACT OF YOUR WORKPLACE SYSTEMS

Workplace systems; now there's a broad phrase. What exactly are we talking about here? In this book, when I say *systems*, I mean the organisational culture and frameworks of people-related processes that exist in, and shape, your workplace and your behaviour in it. As Patrick infers in his quote, a human system is designed to produce particular patterns of behaviour even when no-one is watching, so whether you like it or not, your systems will impact how you lead.

In this chapter we're going to consider two critical systems, culture and people processes, and their potential impact on you.

WHAT CULTURE ARE YOU LEADING IN?

Let's start with the most impactful system of all: culture. Culture is simply 'the way we do things around here'. You can't see it, but you can feel it. You'll discover it in the unwritten rules that govern how people behave in your business. Your first experience of your organisational culture may have been through your interview process when you joined. How was that? Warm and welcoming? Cool and aloof? Sugar coated and cringe-worthy?

Pragmatic and down to earth? Every organisation has a culture, whether the CEO or business owner intended to or not.

Workplace culture is a fascinating topic, and we could spend the rest of the book discussing it, but I just want to give you the nutshell. Culture is formed by the *lived* values and associated behaviours of the leaders and how they encourage others to behave. I emphasise 'lived' because the values that are hanging on the wall behind reception do not influence culture if they are not the ones that are being demonstrated and encouraged every day.

Given that culture is driven by values, I hope your personal values align with your organisation's values and it feels like a comfortable fit. If that's the case for you, you're already off to a good start. As you draw on your personal values to lead people, you will find you're in strong alignment with your company culture and it will support your leadership efforts.

But what if your personal values are at odds with the organisation's values? That can feel very uncomfortable. When the culture encourages us to lead at odds with our personal values, we may have a strong sense of inner dis-ease. This is values misalignment.

Dealing with misaligned values

What can you do if you find your values are misaligned?

First, be clear on what you can influence and what you can't. You *can* influence what happens in your team. You may be able to lead your team in alignment with your values, even if they are different to the values of the organisation you work for. This may go well, or it may not – give it a try to see what happens.

If it goes well you may see your team really lift and become happier and more productive and start to become a beacon of light inside the organisation, and everyone else will be asking, 'How did you do that?' And if that happens, perhaps you have the opportunity to reshape the values throughout your organisation.

If it goes poorly, and you find yourself working for an organisation or a leader where it becomes more difficult for your team to operate, what do you do then? Recently I asked Simon Sinek at a conference I was attending what he would advise a new leader to do if they found themselves in this situation. He said, 'I say learn. To work for a ... leader ... [where your values are out of step] is fantastic school conditions. You will learn so much how NOT to do things and when certain decisions are made how they ripple through the organisation. And how you have one or two leaders within the organisation who are fantastic and you see how they manage. Go to school!'

Good advice. Use this as a learning opportunity. You can add all these learnings to what my husband calls your 'Book of What Not to Do'. I call this type of learning a 'free kick'. You watch someone else's mistakes and learn from them without having to make the same mistakes yourself. And guess what? You're already further ahead with your learning.

And when you feel you've exhausted your learnings, or the disconnect between your values and the values of your organisation becomes too much, it's time to go searching for an organisation where you feel there is a strong alignment between their and your values, so when you join it feels like your hand has just slipped into a nice, warm, well-fitting glove.

WHAT ARE YOUR PEOPLE PROCESSES LIKE?

Now that we've had a look at culture, let's jump into some of the more technical systems at work, things like your recruitment and selection process, induction process, your training and development system, and your performance cycle. These processes support the employee life cycle.

The employee life cycle

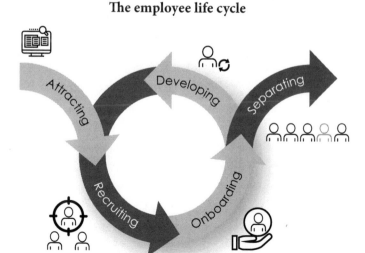

How might these processes impact your people leadership, and what might you do if you discover they are less than ideal?

People processes come in all sorts of different shapes and sizes, some good, some not so good, and in some organisations – particularly new ones and small businesses – there may be very few processes, if any. The challenge for you as a new people leader is to understand how to lead well with the processes you have.

Good people processes

If you're fortunate enough to have good people processes in your workplace, they should help guide and reinforce enabling leadership behaviours. Make sure you take time to understand the processes in place and how they impact you and your team and clarify any questions with your leader. In larger organisations you may be able to access a supportive HR person or business partner to clarify people-related processes and how they apply to you and your team. Good processes save you reinventing the wheel, and when you're learning to lead, they offer a tried-and-tested way of doing things well. As you come along with a fresh set of eyes, remember to flag any suggestions or improvements you might see, so there is continuous improvement of the processes in your organisation.

Poor people processes

This is a tricky one! And unfortunately, not uncommon. It's very challenging when you work in an organisation where the processes appear to *prevent* you from leading your people in the best possible way. Development processes in many organisations can be woefully inadequate – even in those organisations that have a development focus. The most typical thing I hear, which makes me cringe, is, 'When we have our annual review with our team members ...' which translates as, 'Once a year we sit down with our people and do a "tick and flick" exercise to see whether they've completed their mandatory training. And if we can keep that conversation to five minutes, so much the better!' Now picture me with my eyes rolling and exhaling a long, deep, sad sigh.

So perhaps like me you have a deep disregard for superficial processes which don't serve our people, but at the same time you must complete the annual review. If this is the situation you're facing, what do you do? Firstly, think about what you can and cannot control. You can have that 'annual' conversation at the specified time, so you will have completed that obligation. But you can add in other things that make the conversation rich and serve your team members well.

If the evaluation form only has a section on 'training completed this year', you can have additional discussions about their aspirations and development (more on that later!). You can still schedule regular development discussions with your team members and capture your notes and actions separately, and simply provide a consolidated report in the 'annual review form'. So, you've completed your obligation as set out in your poor organisational process, but you have also supplemented what you are doing with your people so they have a better experience and you are being a better leader. I don't think I've ever heard of anyone getting into trouble for having too many development conversations with their team members!

If you're feeling brave, you could have a chat with your leader or someone else in the business who has influence over that process and provide your improvement suggestions. Think creatively and laterally; how might you fulfil your obligations in the process *and* be an exceptional people leader?

If the poor processes inside your organisation are highly constricting and actually prevent you from being the leader you want to be and you've tried to change them and they won't budge, then perhaps it's time to take your learnings of 'what not to do' from your current organisation and move onto another one that is a better fit for you and more aligned with your leadership philosophy.

No or few people processes

If you work in a new or small business, there may be few policies and procedures which influence how you lead your people. This can be both helpful and unhelpful. Helpful; in that you have free rein and get to choose how you lead. Unhelpful; in that perhaps you'd like a little more guidance as you get your head around how to lead people well. In this situation, there are two things you can do. Firstly, refer back to your company values (where they exist) and ask yourself whether you are acting in accordance with these values? If you are, great! If not, what might you need to do differently? Secondly, I'd recommend a conversation with your leader around expectations. You might like to consider asking some of the following questions:

- When I'm making people-related decisions, what particular things would you like me to keep in mind?
- What types of people-related decisions do I need to refer to you?
- When I'm undertaking people processes, who else should I involve?

Getting the answers to these questions will help clarify the road ahead and ensure that you and your leader are working in alignment.

DRA learning reflection

Discoveries:
- Culture and people processes influence how you lead your people.
- Good processes support good leadership and save you time by not having to reinvent the wheel.
- Poor processes can make things tricky, but are not insurmountable.
- Where there are few processes, or no processes, ensure you are clear on expectations by talking with your leader.
- Look for what you can and can't influence and make improvements in the areas that you can influence.

Reflection questions:
- On a scale of 1 to 10, with 1 low and 10 high, how would you rate your organisation's people processes?
- How clear are you about the expectations that your leader has of you?
- How clear are you generally about the things that are within your control?
- What might you do differently to spend more time focusing on the things you can control, and less on the things that you can't?
- What's one thing, within your control, that you could do to improve the people processes in your organisation?

Actions to choose from:

- When I'm following people processes, instead of just following them blindly, I will look for opportunities to improve how we do things.
- When I'm unclear on expectations, instead of just assuming what they might be, I will arrange a conversation with my leader to clarify what they actually are.
- When I discover process issues, instead of trying to fix everything, I will assess which ones are within my control and focus on resolving those issues first.

'When someone says no to a request, they usually mean "not right now" or "not in that way." Most people want to help others, but there are many priorities competing for our time … Don't take it personally. Ask again later. Ask differently.'

James Clear

Chapter 4

BUILDING A STRONG SUPPORT CREW

The great news is that you don't have to do this learning alone. In fact, you'd be mad if you tried to do this solo – leadership is a team sport after all. Time to assemble your support crew. In this chapter we're going to have a look at all the different types of people you can choose from as you select your capable crew who you can call on to guide, support and coach you as you learn to lead.

One thing to consider as you work through this chapter is that opposites are complementary. If you select lots of people who are just like you, guess what you'll get? Lots of opinions and perspectives just like yours. That's great if you just want them to affirm what you already know, but that's not really the point of a support crew. Their mission is to help you learn and grow and support you on the path. Hopefully they will challenge you and 'hurt your brain' just a little, as a friend of mine says.

One of my previous managers, Sharon, was in an executive role and met regularly with the company board. She recalled that she found one of the board members particularly challenging. They always seemed to look at things differently to her and she was finding this frustrating. Then one day, after discussing this issue with her coach, she realised that she could think about this quite differently. She could view the board member's challenges as bringing a different, and useful, perspective that she had not previously considered. This then added value by shifting and broadening her view.

I'd encourage you to actively select a few 'challengers' into your support crew to get the benefit of their opposite and complementary wisdom.

YOUR LEADER

When your leader is leading well, they will be focused on enabling you (and your peers) to be successful. If they achieve this then they too have been successful; after all, that's what being a people leader is all about – enabling our people to be successful, yes?

But what if they're not? What if they feel like more of a hindrance than a help; what then?

In this scenario you have the opportunity for more development 'free kicks'. If your leader continuously creates entries for The Book of What Not to Do, simply watch and learn and then do the opposite. You will be surprised just how helpful that can be to your own growth. And in the meantime, keep an eye out for leaders who inspire you and who demonstrate positive people leadership behaviours.

YOUR PEERS

People Mastery is a small business, and I am so fortunate to be surrounded by the most incredible group of colleagues. We have our commonalities and our unique differences, and while our knowledge overlaps in many places it also differs in interesting ways. For me, my colleagues are the most wonderfully supportive resource. When I tap into my colleagues for support it's like walking into a welcoming, cosy library full of wisdom, where books fly miraculously off the shelves and open themselves in front of me and happen to be 'just right' for the issue I'm facing.

I hope they view my support in the same way.

How well do you know your colleagues? In large organisations, sometimes we can become so focused on the team we lead that we overlook the other important team we're a member of; the team led by our leader that consists of us and our peers. Our peers bring different wisdom and experience, and may even come from quite a different background, and therefore they can provide quite a different and valuable perspective on an issue you might be considering. If you don't know your colleagues so well yet, set up some short catch ups over a coffee or a cup of tea – virtual or face to face – and get to know them better. Start by asking or sharing how *you* might be able to support *them*.

YOUR TEAM

When you begin your journey into people leadership, your primary thought may be that you are there to support your team. Correct, you are. And at the same time your team is also there to support you. Or at least they can be if you ask them.

Think of it this way: your team members are likely the people you interact most with over the course of a day, and they see you warts and all, whether you like it or not! They are in an exceptional position to see your strengths and challenges, and they are well aware of the impact of them.

Enlist their support. Share with them what you're working on – your improvement areas – and ask them for specific help; what can they do to support you? When you're trying to do something new or take a different approach, share with them your intention – what you're doing and why – and then ask them to support you. They may have some suggestions you hadn't even thought of.

ROLE MODELS

Role models are a wonderful support to our growth. Do you know who yours are? If you're fortunate, perhaps you are surrounded by people you aspire to be like. That inspiring leader, that supportive colleague, or even that person outside your work setting who continues to 'set the standard' as you see it. It's also fascinating that our role models don't have to be people we actually know; perhaps they are people you know *of*. In this way anyone, past or present, can be a role model.

When you think of the people leader you would like to become, and hold that vision in your mind's eye, who do you feel currently embodies that vision? Then, as you think of these people, what do you notice about them? How are/were they being? What are/were they doing? Can you break down their being-ness and doing-ness into a few key chunks?

Maybe it's their ability to connect with people around them, maybe it's their ability to articulate clearly where they're headed, maybe it's their ability to listen deeply to you and your challenges. Whatever it might be, these elements are something to which you aspire, and now you have particular behaviours to focus on for your own development. Reviewing our role models can provide us with some key insights on next development steps for ourselves.

ELDERS/MENTORS

I feel very fortunate to have participated in a development program about First Nations people taught by Anny Druett. As a new Australian with Scottish heritage, I have always wanted to build my understanding of Australia's First Nations people as they have such ancient and rich wisdom and culture. Anny taught me many things, and one of the particular things that resonated with me was my learning about Elders. Prior to the training I knew that in Indigenous communities there are lots of Elders, but what I came to learn was that they are Elders in particular subject matter. You might have an Elder who's really knowledgeable about bush tucker, or an Elder who's very knowledgeable about education, and so on. All of the Elders are available to the members of that mob, and what you need to learn will determine which Elder you need to call on for support. I reflected on how incredible it is that these peoples invented the world's first mentoring system over 60,000 years ago!

I love the way our Indigenous culture operates without hierarchy, though not without order, and how it is clear whom one may call on for advice within a particular community. I'd encourage you to bring this thinking to your own community. What might you need advice and support on, and who would be the best person, experienced in this area, to call on? You don't have only one Elder; you have different Elders for different topics. So, think about who you can draw on and build your very own circle of Elders.

COACHES

When you think about successful people in the sporting arena, what do they all have in common? They all have a coach!

(If you've jumped straight to thinking of one of those coaches who stands on the sidelines and yells, red faced, at their team – well, NOT them! Think maybe of the calm and professional tennis coaches who sit quietly observing in the coach's box as their player sweats it out on the court.)

As we'll discover later in the book, when I use the word 'coach' I have a very specific meaning, but at this point just open your mind to the possibility of having someone you can call on who can listen deeply to your opportunities and challenges, provoke your thinking through questioning and enable you to find solutions to your own problems, while maintaining a calm space in which you can undertake this reflective work.

Sound like a powerful tool for growth? Yep, it is!

You may be able to access coaches in your organisation, or you may consider working with your own professional coach external to your organisation. Having developed my own coaching practice over the last eight years, I am always inspired by the insights that can surface in a coaching session. When a person is invited into a calm, reflective space and has the opportunity to consider thoughtful questions on their chosen focus area, so many possibilities can be unlocked.

Leadership tip: a panel of experts

I have one final tip for you on assembling your support crew that comes from the coaching world. Many times, when I'm working one-on-one with a client and they're feeling a bit stuck, or lost with an issue, I ask them to assemble a panel of experts to support them to work through the problem. Obviously, they wouldn't be able to go and grab three people right there and then and bring them into the session, but they can do this action conceptually. Try it.

Step 1: Think of three people whose wisdom and advice you would really value. They can be people known to you like family, friends or colleagues. Or people who you respect from afar like thought leaders in your field (who you know of, but may not know personally), media influencers or global leaders. Interestingly, they can be alive or dead, which means you can select from a vast pool of people.

Step 2: With your issue in mind, and considering each person individually, reflect on what advice you think each person would give you on this issue. As you take turns stepping into each of their shoes to consider your challenge, what different perspectives on your issue emerge?

Step 3: From the different perspectives you've now uncovered, select the best option to move forward on your issue.

I never cease to be amazed by the clarity this exercise can bring to an issue which seemed so challenging. When you use the panel of experts process, you instantly have access to a global support crew who didn't even know they were helping you. Cool, hey?

As we wrap up this chapter, you will now have identified a stellar support crew that you can call on for wisdom and support. Make sure you take the opportunity to seek their assistance and guidance regularly.

This concludes part I. By now you will have completed a thorough review of:

- how to learn
- where you are now in terms of your mindset, beliefs and values
- the culture and systems you're operating in
- the support crew you can draw on for support.

DRA learning reflection

Discoveries:

- Your teachers can teach you both 'what to do' and 'what not to do'. Both learnings are useful.
- Your peers are often an underutilised team of teachers. Use them more.
- Share your strengths and challenges with your team and ask them to help and support you.
- Role models, past or present, provide us with insights and inspiration.
- Elders can specialise in different subject areas. You have many Elders with deep wisdom.
- Coaches can help you unlock new perspectives through powerful questioning.

Reflection questions:

- Who has complementary knowledge, skills and experience to you in your peer group that you could learn from?
- Who are your role models? What can they teach you?
- How might your team members support you in your learning and growth?
- Who are your Elders? What expertise and wisdom do they hold?

Actions to choose from:

- When I'm working on a development issue, instead of just doing it the way I've always done it, I'll think of one of my role models and ask myself, 'What would they do in this situation?', so I can take a different perspective.
- When I'm struggling with a challenge, instead of going round in circles on my own, I will contact at least one of my support crew.
- When I'm overwhelmed, instead of keeping all my challenges to myself, I'll ask, 'Who else in my team could help me with this?'

'The role of a coach is to help others think differently and act upon it'.
Chip McFarlane

Part II

GET SET

Amber light: get set. Amber is an interesting place to be … in between. It's a transition, isn't it? You're in a transition too, right now – between your previous role and fully stepping into the fabulous people leader you're becoming.

This part is all about who you will be as a leader. You're going to transition from being an advice-giving expert to being a people leader with a coaching approach. In this part we'll have a good look at what coaching is and isn't, and how you'll bring a coaching approach to your leadership. Then we'll dive into the three key coaching components; presence, listening and questioning.

You're going to love it.

Let's go!

'Tell less and ask more. Your advice is not as good as you think it is.'
Michael Bungay Stanier

Chapter 5

DEVELOPING YOUR COACHING APPROACH

Back in my role as Manager People & Culture for Snowy Hydro in the late noughties, I remember attending my very first coach training program. It was to be the first of many I undertook on my journey to becoming an Executive Coach. It was day 1, 9 am, and I was standing in a wood-panelled conference room in Sydney alongside my fellow learners, making nervous chit chat as we rolled up our sleeves for the three-day Level 1 coaching program. Our facilitator, Dr Hilary Armstrong, a Master Coach with decades of experience, invited us to consider our current coaching capability. She drew a horizontal scale of 1 to 10 in the air to her left and right, and asked us to place ourselves somewhere on that virtual line. We all looked at each other, trying to gauge comparatively where we should place ourselves without any idea of the others' skills and abilities. After a few moments, we shuffled to Hilary's right-hand side and placed ourselves in different positions between about 6 and 9.

'Well, that's a pretty good start!' she said, with a wry smile on her face.

As the program progressed over the next few days, my learning and understanding of coaching followed an almost vertical learning curve. I was so engaged and absorbed as Hilary kindly, yet firmly, dismantled piece by piece what I thought coaching *was* and created a new and vastly improved understanding of what coaching *is* and how to do it well.

At the end of the program, we were again asked to consider our current coaching capabilities and place ourselves back on that virtual scale of 1 to 10. You can guess what happened next, can't you? We looked at each other, knowing our colleagues and about coaching far more deeply than we could have possibly imagined on day 1, gave a collective eye roll, and swiftly moved down to the lower end of the scale. A knowing and comfortable chuckle emerged from the group; Hilary had deftly put us in our place.

I share this story of my own journey to becoming a coach, the first of very many steps, as a bit of a red flag for you. The words 'coaching' and 'coach' are used a lot in most organisations. It can mean a lot of different things; and often it's not actually coaching. So let's get clear on what I mean when I use the word 'coaching'.

WHAT *IS* COACHING?

Coaching is the ability to enable another person to explore and resolve an issue *for themselves*. Coaches do this work by being present, listening deeply and asking powerful questions. (*Spoiler alert: there is no 'advice giving' component in coaching!*)

I had the opening quote for part II ('The role of a coach is to help others think differently and act upon it') etched into my memory by Chip, another amazing facilitator, on a subsequent coaching program. It's a powerful phrase. If you have a coaching conversation and the coachee leaves the conversation thinking the same way they did when they started, you have not served them well. Your role as a coach is to help them identify and explore different perspectives. We use questions to help us do this work. There is no need to provide advice. The coachee is perfectly capable of coming up with alternate perspectives all by themselves when you ask useful questions.

The second part of the phrase 'act upon it' is just as important. If the coachee takes no action following a coaching session, again we have not served them well. Coaching is not just a rich conversation, it is a rich conversation which leads directly to tangible behaviour change, action and results.

Now that we've clarified what coaching is and what it isn't, maybe you've discovered that you really are coaching and that you're doing it well. Or, perhaps like me, you *thought* you were doing it really well at a 7 to 10 level, where in reality you're more a 1 or a 2. We're going to explore what it *really* means to *take a coaching approach* in your leadership. You'll notice I didn't say 'what it really means to *be a coach*'. Let's dig into why I make that distinction a little more.

UNDERSTANDING THE DIFFERENCE BETWEEN 'COACHING' AND A 'COACHING APPROACH'

After you've read part II of the book, I hope that you, like me, will be capable of coaching one of your team members. We shall have that in common. There is one very important difference though. When I coach my clients, I am *only* their coach. You, on the other hand, are not just your team members' coach. Oh no no no, your world is *a lot* more complicated than mine! You are also always their leader. And not only that. You may also at times be their:

- trainer
- project manager
- support person
- advice giver
- barrier remover.

This is going to feel like you are wearing multiple hats ... which you are. You are going to have to become a competent 'hat switcher' (*that's a technical term!*), knowing which hat you need to be wearing at which time. Just as there is little point wearing a sun hat when it's pouring rain, there's no point wearing the 'advice giver' hat when the person is more than capable of solving their own problem; your 'coaching' hat would be far more appropriate.

When you're learning to coach, be really mindful of the hats you're wearing and try and remove as many as you possibly can before you begin; if you can get down to two hats ('leader' and 'coach'), you'll be doing really well. Even if you're just having a five-minute coaching conversation with a team member, see if you can hang some of those extra hats on your metaphorical hat stand before you begin. Worst-case scenario: you might have several hats stacked on top of each other.

This then is the distinction between 'being a coach' (one hat only: 'coaching') and 'bringing a coaching approach to your leadership' ('leader' hat + 'coaching' hat + other hats). There may be opportunities for you to be only a coach, which provides such freedom. For example, if you're coaching someone outside your organisation, or someone with whom you have no vested interest in their outcome. But when you are coaching your team members you cannot solely be the coach, as the behaviour changes they make and the actions they choose to take will, more often than not, have a direct impact on you and the rest of your team.

So how then does what I'd call 'pure coaching' and 'a coaching approach' look different in practice? Interestingly, to begin with, they won't; they'll look the same. You'll use awesome coaching questions to help the person identify the issue they're working on and where they're at, then you'll ask questions to help them figure out what the possible options are to move forward. Then you'll start to bring your team member to specific actions to wrap up their conversation. This is just what a pure coach would do. The difference is that as their leader, you may have information you need to provide, guidance that you could offer, actions you could also take to support your team member, and more that you ADD into the conversation. This is where you are adding in some of your own wisdom and advice to the conversation. And this is perfectly reasonable when you're wearing the 'leader' *as well as* the 'coach' hat. Pure coaching does not involve providing advice; this is the difference.

The trap here for new leaders is they hear 'you'll be doing a bit of both' and, unfortunately, they don't stick with the coaching process for long enough in the conversation and, in the end, they just keep on providing advice and the team member gets a raw deal. My challenge to you is to act like a pure coach. Use your 'questions only' approach until the team member just can't come up with anything else – literally question them to exhaustion! I don't mean until they fall asleep. I just mean until they cannot think of any more ideas or suggestions to move forward. When, and only when, you have exhausted all their ideas may you add your own. And when you're doing this well, it will become rarer and rarer for you to have to add your own ideas as you'll realise they've come up with a far better suggestion that you would have by themselves. And that my friend is coaching GOLD! Surround yourself with people who are smarter than you, right?!

Given that this 'giving advice' business is the biggest trap for new people leaders when they're learning how to coach, I think we should talk about why stepping back from giving advice is so important.

WHY WON'T I BE GIVING ADVICE WHEN I'M COACHING?

Let's create a theoretical example from your world first to understand a little more about why you won't be giving advice when you're coaching.

Picture one of your own leaders. It could be someone who used to lead you, or it could even be your current leader. You contact them to see if they can spare some time to help you on a particular challenge you're facing. When you catch up with them and share the issue you're grappling with, a few pennies start dropping as you talk it through, and you start to see a glimmer of an idea about how you might move forward. While this glimmer takes shape, your leader is listening, and then as you share your thoughts further, they start interjecting with ...

- 'Yeah, but I think you should really do this ...', or ...
- 'You know what I did when I was in that situation? I did ...', or ...
- 'Don't you think that it would be better if you ...', or ...
- 'Look, I hear what you're saying, but that's not going to work because ...'

While hearing from their experience at times can be useful, how do you feel when this is *all* they offer?

- Frustrated? *Because they're not really giving your ideas any airtime.*
- Annoyed? *Because they seem to think that all their ideas are better than yours.*
- Disappointed? *Because they don't seem to think you have the ability to work it out for yourself.*
- Resentful? *Because they don't think your ideas have any merit.*
- Resigned? *Because *eye roll* this is always how these conversations go. I don't even know why I bother coming up with my own ideas as I always*

end up with one of their solutions. I'll just get back in my box and keep my ideas to myself ...

Not pretty, is it? If every time you go to your leader to work through an issue you're facing you only receive their advice on how to fix it, what happens? You stop thinking for yourself, as your ideas (obviously) aren't good enough and you become dependent on that leader.

If you're having that slightly uncomfortable, squirmy-in-the-tummy feeling as you replay your last few days at work and remember the constant stream of interruptions from your team members asking you for your advice, and you then telling them exactly how things are to be done ... you're not alone. It's a common trap for emerging leaders. But together we're going to sort out that problem, once and for all! 'Bring it on!', you say? Okay then, let's go!

HOW DO I BRING A COACHING APPROACH TO MY LEADERSHIP?

Remember earlier I mentioned that coaches do their work by being present, listening deeply and asking powerful questions? Yes? (*Awesome work – paying attention!*) Well, that's exactly how you're going to apply this coaching approach to your wonderful work as a leader.

Being present is the 'secret sauce' of your coaching approach, and in our constantly interrupted worlds can be the most challenging element to master. Then comes deep listening; tuning in to not only what is said, but what is meant by the person you're listening to. Finally, you will be using questions to support your team member to unravel challenges, explore opportunities, change their behaviour and implement actions that will bring success.

In the following three chapters, I'll build your understanding of what these three different elements of coaching are, and how to apply them in your everyday work.

Let's get into it.

DRA learning reflection

Discoveries:
- Becoming a leader involves letting go of advice giving and applying a coaching approach.
- Coaching enables your team members to find their own solutions to their challenges.
- As a people leader you wear the 'leader' and 'coach' hats at the same time.
- New leaders often fall into the trap of adding in their advice to the conversation too early.
- Taking a coaching approach with your team builds their confidence and independence.
- Great coaching involves being fully present, deep listening and curious questions.

Reflection questions:
- Currently, when a team member comes to you with an issue, how do you generally respond?
- How might you ask more questions of your team members?
- How might you frame your advice differently (when eventually you do provide it) so it becomes an option rather than a direction?
- Who do you know who acts like a coach? What questions do they ask?
- In which situations do you find yourself more able to act like a coach, and less like an advice giver?

Actions to choose from:

- When one of my team comes to me with an issue, instead of instantly providing advice, I'll ask them three questions to help them explore the issue themselves first.
- When one of my team comes to me for advice, instead of providing the answer, I'll ask them, 'What do you think might be the best way to move forward with this?'
- When I need to provide advice to a team member, instead of providing it like a direction, I'll say, 'I have another option you might consider ...' before providing my suggestion.

'Nothing is more important than being in the present moment. Fully alive. Fully aware.'

Thich Nhat Hanh

Chapter 6

UNDERSTANDING AND USING PRESENCE

KEEPING IT PRACTICAL

No, not presents (*you wish!*), but presence! Well, actually, presence means being fully *in* the present, so you're kinda right! Are you starting to freak out and hear Buddhist chanting and the sound of panpipes in your mind …? Don't fret, we're going to keep this really practical. That said, if you're a fan of meditation and mindfulness and have some existing daily practices in place, you'll already be a few steps ahead on this one and you can bring those practices to your coaching.

For those of you for whom 'being present' is a new thing, or a thing you struggle with, basically, being present in this situation means being fully tuned into your team member while you're having your coaching conversation.

Imagine you're going to see a movie at the cinema that you can't wait to see …

You find your seat, and make sure you have a great view of the screen. You're sitting comfortably. And as the movie starts, you're surrounded by the music, the dialogue and the pictures. You're engrossed in the story that's being played out for you, and your attention is purely here and now in the movie. You're not thinking about what's for dinner later, you're not checking your phone, you're not chatting to your buddy. You don't have to provide artistic direction to the director. You are simply listening and observing. You are fully 'in' the movie.

I went to see *The Dry* with the fabulous Eric Bana. The storyline was quite challenging (there were multiple murders) but during the movie, I felt like I was 'in it'. Totally absorbed. And this is the feeling you should have when you are present with your team members. You should have your eyes and ears, heart and mind fully tuned into the team member you are working with:

- Eyes – what am I observing/not observing?
- Ears – what are they saying/not saying?
- Heart – what might they be feeling/not feeling?
- Mind – what might they be thinking/not thinking?

This sounds fairly full on, right? It can be difficult. As with anything that's worth doing well, becoming really good at being present with your team members is going to take practice. Here are six things you can do to help you be more present:

1. Find the right time.
2. Find a suitable location.
3. Set your intention.
4. Remove digital distractions.
5. Notice and manage your wandering attention.
6. Ask for feedback.

Let's look at each of these elements in a little more detail.

Find the right time

Your team member asks you, 'Hey, do you have time for me to bounce an idea around with you for five minutes?' In that split second before you respond, you may experience some, if not all, of these competing thoughts:

- Uh ohhhh! I know they're saying 'five minutes', but these things always run over and I've got so much on ...

- I really want to say 'yes', but I'm supposed to be in that presentation in 10 minutes – shall I try to squeeze it in?
- Team member or my boss's request? Team member or my boss's request? Team member or my boss's request?

Sound familiar? All of the thoughts above are going to impact your ability to be present. And yet, you feel that really you should be making time to talk with your team member, so what do you do?

Just take a breath and ask them, 'How long do you really think this conversation will take?' Whatever answer they provide, whether it's 10 minutes, 30 minutes or two hours, ask yourself when that conversation could realistically happen in the time you currently have available so that you could be fully present. If it's not now, then you could say:

> Look, I really want to be able to give you my full attention when we catch up, and currently I'm focusing on [insert your upcoming meeting/current work/issue] at the moment. Can we look at our diaries and see when the next best time for us would be to talk about this and lock in some time please?

Now your team member knows you want to seriously listen to what they have to say, and you've made time in your diary to do that. Super!

If, on the other hand, you tried to squeeze their two-hour conversation request into the 10-minute window you have in your diary now, your mind will keep skipping off to your next meeting. As you sit there worrying that you'll end up running late, your mind is somewhere else and your presence has evaporated.

You might also like to think about times of the day or times in the week when you find it easier to be present, and let your team know when those general times are. You can also think about whether you're a morning person or an afternoon person, or perhaps you're a just-after-lunch person.

When generally do you find it easiest to be present?

Find a suitable location

Think about where would be best to hold this conversation. Are you standing together in a busy corridor as people are bustling past? Are you trying to talk at the side of a worksite as noisy equipment drowns out your conversation? Or are you trying to talk in a hectic kitchen with everyone else within earshot?

If you're going to be present for your team member, you need to find a space that's going to make that easier for you. What about a quiet corner of the office with a couple of comfy chairs? Or side by side in your ute, which offers you a chance to block out some of the noise of your worksite? Or the park across the road from your cafe where you can have a quiet chat on a park bench? There are many places you can go that enable you to tune out what's going on around you and tune in directly to what your team member is saying.

Where is the best place you could go when you want to be fully present with your team member?

Set your intention

Before you meet with your team member, take a few minutes to yourself to set your intention for your conversation:

- *How do you want to be in the conversation?* Present. Focusing only on them. Really trying to understand their perspective/challenge/ opportunity/concern.
- *What do you need to let go of before the conversation?* The previous conversations you've been in during the day and all the actions that are crowding your mind.
- *How would you like your team member to feel during and after your conversation?* Like they were deeply listened to and felt truly heard.

Sometimes it takes a few minutes to change gears from what you've been doing previously to the conversation you're going to have next with your team member, so taking a few minutes to set your intention prior to your discussion can be very helpful. If you happen to have fallen into the trap of having back-to-back-to-back meetings in your diary, this can be a significant derailer to intention setting. Try booking meetings for 25 minutes instead of 30, or 50 minutes instead of an hour, to allow you to build in some intention-setting time.

You may also find it useful to link this intention-setting practice to another existing behaviour that you already have in place. Perhaps before you go into a discussion you refill your water bottle. If so, while you're filling your water bottle, reset your intention for your discussion.

Remove digital distractions

Something super easy you can do to help you be more present with your team member is remove all your potential digital distractions.

Firstly, put your phone on silent and either place it face down or even better put it somewhere you can't see it. Now, hold on, I know what you're thinking, *I thought she said this was an easy one?? Letting go of my phone … I don't know if I can …* You can do this! You really can. (*I'm saying this with my tongue firmly lodged in my cheek!*)

Seriously though, I reckon my Mum has a really healthy approach with her mobile phone – she says, 'My phone is for my convenience, not everyone else's!' So, channel my Mum (*we might call this the 'Mother Knows Best' principle!*) and park your phone when you're in conversation with your team member. There is nothing worse than being on the cusp of getting a lovely insight from your team member when *beep … beep …* a notification comes through on your phone (or your smart watch if you're fancy!), you glance down, break the connection with your team member and BOOM! … the moment is gone. What a shame. And the notification turns out to be a request to confirm your next dental appointment. Yeah. Awesome.

Secondly, if you're working face to face, I'd suggest moving away from your computer. One of my lovely program participants, Julie, who leads a team at Red Energy's call centre in Melbourne, shared that whenever one of her team members approaches to have a conversation with her, she swivels her chair so that her back is facing her computer screen and she is facing her team member, so that she can't even see her screen in her peripheral vision. She finds it makes such a difference to her ability to be present.

You may have experienced that sinking feeling when you're trying to talk with someone and their eyes keep glancing away from you and you know that they're actually trying to keep an eye on something else. Funny how quickly those kinds of conversations dry up.

Many of you will be working virtually, so what do you do then? You might be on Google Meet, or Teams, or Zoom or [insert your choice of videoconferencing platform here]. My tip is to close all other programs on your computer so that you have only the video conference open together with any other content you need for that specific conversation. Close everything else down. Again, switch off other notifications so you can be present for your team member online. Use a good headset so that you're only hearing them and are not distracted by any other sounds.

Notice and manage your wandering attention

Jack Kornfield, an American author, Buddhist practitioner and teacher, has a lovely analogy for our wandering minds which have difficulty staying present. Think of your last conversation with a team member. Perhaps instead of really being present your mind wandered off to thinking about that evening's dinner options, or your upcoming presentation, or an argument you had with a friend earlier in the day. Jack says that our untrained wandering mind is like a puppy:

> We put the puppy down and say, 'Sit. Stay.' What does it do? It gets up and runs around. 'Stay.' It runs around again. Twenty times, 'Stay.' After a while, slowly, the puppy settles down.

Jack's advice for the times when we notice our 'puppy' has wandered off mid-conversation is to notice that the 'puppy' has gone, and gently and calmly 'bring the puppy back'. I can't tell you how many times I find myself saying 'bring the puppy back', 'bring the puppy back', 'bring the puppy back' during the course of a day. (*I think if my mind were a puppy, it would be a cheeky chocolate Labrador! What would yours be?*)

I find this analogy particularly powerful because if we were training a puppy, we would be gentle, kind and persistent. Sadly, so often when we talk to ourselves we use a frustrated, angry and scolding voice. So, treating ourselves, and our wandering minds, like we would treat a new puppy encourages us to bring compassion to our own learning so we can become more and more present with our team members and others over time.

Ask for feedback

As you practise being present with your team member, ask them for feedback on how you're doing. You could use a question like, 'On a scale of 1 to 10, with 1 low and 10 high, how present was I with you today?' Or even simpler, 'How well did you feel I listened to you today?' When your team member gives you their response, you can follow up with, 'If there was one thing I could do to improve my listening, what would you suggest?' It will be fascinating to see what they say. If you ask each of your team members this question, you may start to notice a pattern or a theme in the feedback; maybe it's 'put your phone down' or 'ask more questions' or 'stop talking over me'.

Then you need to think about how you will implement their suggestions. If you ask for feedback and don't implement it, you might find in the future when you ask for *more* feedback, people are not keen to give it, as they can't see the point because you didn't do anything with it last time.

One interesting reflection I've had while writing this chapter is that when we are fully present, what's actually happening is that we become fully attuned to our team member, or any other person for that matter. Think of it like an old-fashioned radio – you turn the dial trying to find the right station, and as the dial moves there's quite a lot of noisy static, but once you manage to find the correct station, the static disappears and the voice of the presenter comes through crystal clear. We are tuned in to the station.

When you become present you enable your listening to become completely tuned in to your team member.

DRA learning reflection

Discoveries:

- Being present with your team member will have *them* feeling that you're fully tuned in to them.
- Being present with your team member will have *you* fully focused on them and not distractedly thinking about 'other stuff'.
- Setting your intention for each conversation enables you to be more present.
- Digital distractions erode presence.
- When we treat our mind as a playful puppy we can gently 'bring the puppy back' to the present moment.

Reflection questions:

- On a scale of 1 to 10, with 1 low and 10 high, how would you rate your presence with your team right now?
- What might your team members say about your level of presence with them currently?
- When generally do you find it easiest to be present with your team members?
- Where is the best place you could go when you want to be fully present with a team member?
- How might you adjust your diary/schedule to create time for intention setting between meetings?

- What can you do to reduce your digital distractions?
- What might you, kindly and gently, say to yourself when you get distracted to return to presence?

Actions to choose from:

- When I schedule meetings in my diary, instead of running them back to back, I will leave time between meetings to allow me to reset my intention each time.
- When my team member asks me if I have five minutes to discuss something, instead of agreeing without thinking, I will ask, 'What's the issue and how long do you think it really needs for discussion?', and schedule a mutually convenient time for the conversation in our diaries.
- When I meet with a team member, instead of continuing what I'm doing while speaking with them, I will stop what I'm doing and put my phone on silent so I am fully present with them.

'To really listen is to be moved physically, chemically, emotionally, and intellectually by another person's narrative.'

Kate Murphy

Chapter 7

HOW TO LISTEN LIKE A COACH

Deeply listening to your team members is one of the greatest gifts you can offer them. Similar to being present, deep listening takes a lot of practice.

Being present is definitely a prerequisite to deep listening. If you are not present, you are likely listening to something other than your team member. You might be listening to your mind chatter about other work activities you have on your plate, or you might be listening to background noise or another conversation that's happening close by.

Have you ever been having a chat with a few people and then tuned out of the conversation you're in, to listen in to another conversation that's happening in another group? I find myself doing this at parties sometimes. Then you tune back into your own group's conversation and realise it's moved on a few steps and you're not quite sure where it's up to. You then stumble back into the conversation and, like a deaf grandparent, ask something that's already been covered and end up feeling like a bit of a muppet! You'll remember that it can feel very embarrassing.

So, let's explore how to listen deeply and effectively to your team members. Let's see how we can learn to *listen like a coach*!

BEING LISTENING

At the beginning of my coaching career, I worked for several years as a Learning Transfer Coach with Emma Weber. Through Emma's company, Lever Transfer of Learning, I worked with many of Australia's ASX-listed businesses and some global clients to support their leaders to transfer their learning from their training programs back into their daily work. Emma is the most fabulous coach, an exceptional role model and a gifted teacher, and I feel extremely fortunate that I had her to guide the development of my coaching practice. In one of the first learning programs I did with her, she introduced me to the concept of 'being listening'. It might feel a little bit weird right now to think of listening as something you're *being*, as opposed to something you're *doing*. But I share this concept with you as it will really help shift your understanding of what deep listening actually is.

Let's start with the distinction between *hearing* and *listening*.

If you are standing close enough to your team member when they are speaking you will 'hear' what they are saying. Basically, that means the sounds of their words WILL go into your ears. This is not the same as listening to those words though, is it? When you are listening – being present and alert and making an effort to understand something – then when those sounds arrive in your ears you will have the ability to make meaning from what your team member is saying.

And there's more.

When we are 'being listening' we are not just listening with our ears. We are also listening with our eyes. What can you see that adds more meaning to what they are saying? Maybe they look uncomfortable as they share something. Maybe they look relieved. Maybe they look animated. How does this add to what they are saying?

We are also listening with our hearts.

Remember the phrase 'having a heart to heart'? These days you might be more familiar with the term 'having a D&M', a 'deep and meaningful' conversation, which is very similar. A 'heart to heart' is a close conversation where you have a meeting of hearts, not just minds. You might not have thought about having a heart-to-heart conversation with one of your team members, but when you are deeply listening and listening from the heart, this level of conversation and discussion becomes possible. They are most often the conversations where 'a-ha moments' happen.

We are also listening with our bodies.

There are two elements to listening with your body. Let's simply call them 'external' and 'internal'.

External body listening is where you are using your body to demonstrate that you are paying attention. You are turned towards your team member. You are in a relaxed and open pose – arms relaxed, shoulders down, limbs resting and not fidgety. You may lean forward slightly to indicate your interest. You use your facial expressions (like a smile) or your body language (like a nod) to encourage your team member to speak more. They will be able to see that your body is focused towards them. You may even find that when you are really tuned in to your team member that unconsciously your body starts to match the gestures that your team member is making – they lean forward, you lean forward. (It's fun 'people watching' in restaurants to see this happen – some are 'in sync', some are not!)

Internal body listening is where you are using the feelings inside your own body to add to your listening. This might sound a bit weird at first, but I'm pretty sure you'll be able to relate to this example.

A dear friend of mine, Kirsty, has just written her first book. In the lead up to the book launch Kirsty filmed a video trailer to promote the book's release. The day prior to the launch Kirsty was understandably having last-minute jitters about releasing the video onto social media, and asked me to review it. As I clicked 'play' on the video and started to watch Kirsty talk about her book I could feel a tingling sensation running up and down my spine – you know, like positive goosebumps? She spoke so passionately about the topic of her book and my body was echoing my thoughts that Kirsty had 'nailed it'. My body and my mind were in alignment, and I felt certain that Kirsty's message would land well with her intended audience.

If you think back through your own experience, you might be able to recall some situations where your body was telling you that something felt 'right', or perhaps felt 'wrong'. When something feels right, it might feel like tingles or positive goosebumps or even an inner warmth in the centre of your chest. When something feels wrong, it might feel like a tightness in your throat, or a niggle in your gut or even a tightening in your chest or shoulders. Take the opportunity to listen to your body and see what signals your clever body is sending you.

Listening internally for the times when your body and mind are in alignment – it sounds right and feels right, or sounds wrong and feels wrong – and for those times when there is a misalignment – it sounds right, but feels wrong, or vice versa – enables you to listen more holistically (with your WHOLE body) and to dig deeper into the conversation. Set yourself a challenge to notice your listening over the next few days. What might you discover?

Once you've managed to *be* listening, what are you actually listening for?

LEVELS OF LISTENING

When you're having a conversation with a team member you might find yourself listening at a few different levels. There are many models of 'listening levels' out there, and the one I'm going to share with you is nice and simple, and was taught to me on my Level 1 Coaching Program with the Institute of Executive Coaching and Leadership. I'm confident you will be able to relate easily to it and it will really enhance your listening abilities.

I've included a diagram which sets out the different levels. Let's visit each level one by one. We'll start from the outside and work our way in.

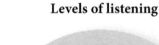

Levels of listening

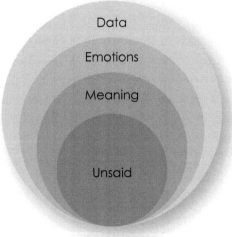

Data

Emotions

Meaning

Unsaid

Data

Most of you will already be able to do this fairly well (*apart from the times when you've slipped into 'deaf grandparent mode'*), as this is when you simply listen to what is being said. What words and information are being shared with you by the team member? While I appreciate that you may understandably think this is what listening is all about, it is only the first level.

Let's imagine you have the following situation:

One of your team members, Jamie, approaches you about some concerns he has about another team member, Jo, whom he believes is being overly critical of the work he is doing. Jamie wrote and circulated a paper on the next stage of the project they're working on and then presented the paper at a meeting this week, about which Jo had five issues. Nobody else had any comments on the paper.

You have a 10-minute conversation with Jamie about the situation. If you were listening only for the data and information, you might hear something like this:

- Jamie presented the paper at a project meeting last Tuesday.
- All the project team were in attendance.
- Jo identified five issues with the paper.
- None of the other project team members raised any issues with Jamie's paper.

Now let's jump into the next level of listening. This is when we're listening for emotions.

Emotions

What do you notice about Jamie's emotions? You may be able to pick this up through his tone of voice, his pace or pitch (you can *hear* the emotion), and when you look hard you may also see some visual clues as to his feelings on this issue through facial expressions or body language (you can *see* the emotion). You may also be able to sense the emotion – this is empathy – through your heart-to-heart connection (you can *feel* the emotion).

When you're listening for emotion, in addition to the data you heard at the first level, you might *also* 'hear' something like this:

- Jamie looks upset – you notice tears forming in the corners of his eyes.
- Jamie is talking quite quickly and loudly about the situation, with his hands on his hips.
- You sense a combination of embarrassment and frustration.

Meaning

If you and I had a dollar for every time we've said or heard the phrase 'I know that's what I said, but that's not what I meant!', I'm sure we'd both be millionaires. What is said (data) and what is meant (meaning) can be very different. When you're listening deeply, your job is to be a listening bloodhound, to try your best to sniff out the meaning behind the words.

Human beings are meaning-making machines; we like to make sense of stuff. When we're a leader, we have a responsibility to discover what our team members mean when they are speaking with us. It's not sufficient to say, 'Yeah, I heard what you said' – in other words, you listened to the words. You must strive for 'I understand what you mean'. Even better, you can check back with your team member to confirm you have the correct understanding:

> Right Jamie, thanks for telling me about that issue. Can I just share back with you what I'm hearing so far and make sure that I really understand what you're saying?

When you do this well, your team member will feel truly heard by you. In my experience, these are magical moments of deep connection. Continuing our conversation above, it may sound something like this:

> Okay Jamie, so all the project team members were happy with your paper, except Jo. It sounds like you're feeling frustrated that Jo would raise five issues with your paper, when everyone else is okay with it. And perhaps you're feeling a little angry or embarrassed about the way Jo handled that in the meeting? Have I got that right?

Unsaid

But wait, there's more!

One more level; the unsaid. As I'm sure you're gathering by now, I love a good metaphor, so here's another one for you: the unsaid can be 'the elephant in room'. You know when there's a great big issue, maybe something controversial and fairly obvious, but it's not being mentioned? As the elephant circles the conversation, you can feel the vibration of its footsteps, you may even hear the deafening silence of it trumpeting from the corner trying to draw attention to itself, but nonetheless it doesn't even get a mention. Not. One. Word. Weird, huh? When you feel there is an elephant in the room, it's definitely *on you* – as the leader – to dig deeper and find out what's going on.

Interestingly, the unsaid is not just about elephants. It can be about something that you expected to come up, but didn't. Or you have a feeling that your team member is skirting around 'something' but you're not sure what. It could be you feel that there is something more they want to say, but you have a sense they are holding back. Listening for the unsaid requires you to be fully present and using your ears, eyes, heart and mind to deduce what's missing from the conversation.

You might explore the unsaid with questions like:

- What have I not asked you yet, that I should ask?
- What else is relevant here?
- I get a sense there's something else you're concerned about here. What might that be?

Putting that in context might sound something like this:

You: Jamie, I notice you're quite upset about this. I'm feeling there's something else underneath this situation that's concerning you. What's the key issue for you in this situation with Jo?

Jamie: Yeah, well it's not that Jo raised issues with my paper – I'm fine with constructive criticism … it's just the way Jo did it in that meeting made me feel a bit humiliated, particularly as we're on the same team. Why didn't Jo just come and talk to me one on one about the issues before the meeting, so I could have resolved them beforehand?

Bingo! Now you've got to the root cause of the issue and now you can work together to resolve it. That's the power of deep listening.

We'll explore some other great questions and strategies you can use to manage tricky situations like these when we come to the next chapter on questions, but before we go there, I'd like to bring a few possible barriers to your listening to your attention.

POSSIBLE BARRIERS TO LISTENING

If we look back at our original levels of listening model, you can see that in the following image there is now an additional ring. This outer ring, which contains these barriers, has a *very* technical term; they are classified under the heading 'My stuff'! These are the things that prevent you from listening for data, emotions, meaning and the unsaid, and alter *how* you are perceiving those things.

Levels of listening

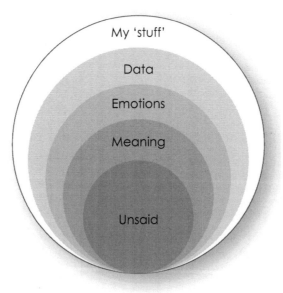

'My stuff' can include all sorts of things. It might be assumptions you hold about the topics being shared, preconceptions about a team member, it might even be a bias you hold – either consciously or unconsciously. It could be some poor listening habits you demonstrate. While none of this stuff is sounding very pretty right now, it's important to examine it so you can build your awareness of your own listening traps and then implement some positive changes. You may have some of these attributes, you may have all of them; either way, I'm pretty confident that even the best coach in the world falls prey to barriers to listening from time to time, and the more aware of them we are, the more quickly you can turn things around.

Yes, but ...

These two very common words – when used on their own – seem completely harmless. When used in combination however, they become one of the most damaging barriers to deep listening. While at this point you're probably wondering, *how on earth could two such simple words possibly take the number one spot in the list of 'most damaging barriers to listening'?* I can assure you that over the last decade the exercise I run in my programs on 'Yes, but ...', which was taught to me by Michael, an engaging and provocative Irishman, is one that participants rate consistently as their most significant learning when it comes to improving their listening.

Hopefully you'll recognise the following situation, or a slight variation on this theme:

Team member: Thanks for making time to talk with me about this upcoming offsite development day we're planning. I was hoping we could bounce around a few ideas about the location?

Leader: Sure thing. No problem at all. What are you thinking?

TM: Well, I was thinking it would be good to have it in a venue near the ocean, so after the session we could have a bit of down time and relax ...

Leader: Yeah, but having the team in the ocean could be a bit of safety risk, I reckon.

TM: Oh, I see. So, maybe we could go up to the mountains instead? There are some awesome walking trails up there that we could do at the end of each day.

Leader: Yes, but it's a bit too far away, we'll burn too much time getting there and back.

TM: Hmmmm, I didn't think of that. What about if we went to the city instead? There are some great hotels with good conference facilities and plenty to do post workshop ... ?

Leader: Yeah, but the city? The traffic's going to be a nightmare ...

TM: *awkward silence*

You can see what's happening here, can't you? 'Yes, but ...' shuts down the conversation. The team member keeps coming up with suggestions and ideas, and each time the 'Yes, but ...' response by the leader slam dunks them into oblivion. Is it any surprise that the team member just gives up in the end?

You'll be amazed just how many times you, your team and your colleagues use the phrase, 'Yes, but ...'. Now that you've read this section, pay close attention to how often this little phrase slips so easily from your lips and watch the impact it has ... you could really classify it as a weapon of mass destruction.

So how do you combat this sneaky wee barrier?

It has a two-word antidote: 'Yes, and ...'

Let's try that scenario again using 'Yes, and...' instead of Yes, but ...'

Team member: Thanks for making time for me to talk with me about this upcoming offsite we're planning. I was hoping we could bounce around a few ideas about the location?

Leader: Sure thing. No problem at all. What are you thinking?

TM: Well, I was thinking it would be good to have it in a venue near the ocean, so after the session we could have a bit of down time and relax ...

Leader: Yeah, that sounds like an interesting option, AND it could be a bit of a safety risk having the team in the ocean I reckon.

TM: Well, we could make sure we have some ground rules, like everyone has to swim between the life-saver's flags, and maybe we have to be in pairs if we're in the water ... ?

Leader: Yes, AND are there any other risks you can think of?

TM: Well, I guess there is the driving risk for the trip. It can be a pretty busy road during summer with caravans and motorbikes, and there's that crazy mountain with all the hairpins to get around.

Leader: Yes, I think you're right, AND how might we overcome that challenge?

TM: I'm thinking we could ... [conversation continues ...]

Notice that using 'yes, and ...' doesn't have to mean you agree with what the person is saying. It's perfectly fine to say:

> Yes, I hear and understand what you're saying AND I have a completely different opinion.

When you just say …

> Yes, but I have a completely different opinion.

… it negates the opinion put forward by your team member.
Your message is *perceived* as:

> Yeah nah (as they say in Australia), I don't think your suggestion is any good. Here's my far better suggestion.

This is quite a neat example of the difference between data and meaning – what you said, versus what you meant.

Try substituting 'Yes, but …' with 'Yes, and …' and watch the ideas of your people bloom, and you will enable them to become more independent.

My colleague, Jillian, and I have a great way of reminding each other about the power of 'Yes, and …' when we are disagreeing and debating something by email. We simply type:

'Yes, AND …'

We type the AND in capital letters. Not to mean that we are shouting, but that we do understand and acknowledge what each other has said, even though we may not agree. Our debate continues until we have an even better idea than either of us individually started with.

This is the power of 'Yes, and …'

Interrupting

I'm grateful to a previous manager of mine, who taught me a valuable lesson about interrupting when I was working with him in the Corporate Services team for the Broken Hill Water Board many moons ago. We had a great working relationship. He was a very experienced corporate services manager who had a passion for developing people and had a fairly direct style, which was great for me as I never had to guess what he was thinking.

One day he called me into his office to discuss an issue. He was sitting behind his desk, which was covered in piles of paperwork, manila folders, notes, journals and the like. I remember feeling really engaged in the discussion as the conversation bounced to and fro between us and then, suddenly, he stopped talking. Just stopped, dead. Right in the middle of the discussion. I was totally perplexed ... what was going on?

'Is everything okay? Why have you stopped talking?' I asked.

'Well, there's not any point of me talking ...' he offered. By now I was feeling completely bamboozled.

'Why not?'

'Because apparently you seem to know everything I'm going to say and you keep interrupting me and finishing my sentences for me!'

He wasn't exactly shirty, but he wasn't really happy either, I can tell you. Fair enough too.

When I sat back and thought about it, yes, I had been engaged. But I had thought that I knew where he was going with the conversation and I had kept jumping in on top of what he was saying before he was finished. Only in hindsight did I realise how annoying that must have been! My enthusiasm and engagement in the conversation had become a blunt instrument. I apologised, and I can't remember now if I thanked him for his valuable feedback, but I sincerely hope I did. I had been completely unaware of this barrier to my listening.

Do you find yourself finishing other people's sentences like me, or jumping in and taking the conversation off in another direction before your team member has had a chance to say everything they *want* to say? I confess that I am still working to improve on this one. I'm definitely better. But every now and again I recognise the red flag that I'm doing this when I've jumped in too early and misinterpreted where someone was heading with the conversation, when I should have just kept my mouth closed and listened. It can sound like this:

Team member: 'And so I was feeling — '

Leader (interrupting):   'Frustrated?'

Team member: 'No. Actually, I was feeling disappointed.'

If you're hearing a 'no' followed by a different response from the one you offered, you might also have fallen victim to the interruption trap.

Tune into the other person's body language and facial expressions. Do they look like they've finished? Allow a few moments after the end of their sentence before adding anything. And if you accidentally talk over them, just apologise and step back into silence and let them finish, or simply invite them to continue. 'I'm sorry I interrupted you. Please, go on,' is all it takes.

Bias

Bias is a fascinating topic. There are many forms of bias, and I think it's important to briefly explore what a bias is and how it can be a barrier to your listening.

Here's a simple way of understanding it: have you ever played lawn bowls? Maybe you've had a fun afternoon of barefoot bowls with your team at a local bowling club at one time or another. If you have, you will know that a lawn bowling ball is weighted; one side of the ball has a greater weight than the other. When you bowl, the balls don't go in a straight line, they curve. They lean to one side.

Figuratively speaking, this is what a bias does to your mind. A bias causes your mind to lean to one 'side'. Biases are similar to prejudices. Sadly, you may be quite familiar with some of the common prejudices in our society like racism, sexism and ageism, where people mistakenly believe that one race is better than another, one gender is better than another or one age group is better than another.

But for our purposes, in terms of barriers to listening, let's focus on one particular bias called 'confirmation bias'. Confirmation bias is the tendency of people to favour information that confirms or strengthens their own existing beliefs or values. It's an information processing 'glitch' if you like, where we are filtering or sifting what we're hearing to confirm what we *think* we know. The challenging thing about biases is that they can be unconscious, meaning we don't know that we have them, which can make them very tricky to remove.

So, what does confirmation bias mean for our listening? Well, it means that when we're listening, we can be unconsciously listening selectively. Your brain listens for information that confirms your own understanding or interpretation of events. Perhaps you're listening to your team member and you think or say, 'A-ha! That's what *I thought*!' You believe the person is confirming the information you already had on the subject. When we're listening, we must focus on listening openly, and when we have awareness of confirmation bias that can help us choose to listen for disconfirming evidence in a situation. We can even choose to directly ask for information that is contrary to our thoughts on a situation. For example, 'What do you think is wrong with my idea?'

When we are aware of the existence of bias, then we can work to actively challenge ourselves to listen for new information, and particularly information that is contrary to our own views, and thereby hear the full picture.

Assumptions

You know what they say about assumptions, don't you? 'When you assume you make an ASS of U and ME!' Assumptions are another common barrier to listening. Have you ever been listening to one of your team members and found yourself thinking ...

- I know exactly where this is going.
- They're saying that because ...
- They're feeling that way because ...

And therein lies the danger of making assumptions. You *think* you know. So, while you may have physically heard 30% of the issue from your team member, you've filled the remaining 70% of your 'understanding' of the situation with your assumption from your own experience or knowledge. Because you've been there. You've done that task. You've faced that challenge. You've overcome that problem before. So, you *know*. And what they're talking about is exactly the same as your situation in the past, right? WRONG.

When we make assumptions about what someone is saying, it takes us straight to advice giving, doesn't it?

Oh, when that happened to me, I did X. So, you should do X, too.

You think that you can just tell them how to deal with their situation. This closes off your listening and then switches you from coaching to advice giving. Instead of making assumptions and jumping to conclusions and then jumping to giving advice, try asking more questions to help your team member uncover all the different aspects of the situation, and then ask them questions to help them figure out some options to move forward. (More on how specifically to do this in the next chapter.)

Too busy

But what if you're too busy to listen to your team member right now?

Not having enough time is a common barrier to listening. In the chapter on presence, we looked at how to make sure you are giving your team members the time they deserve, in a way that works for both of you.

Remember that you can reschedule and share your intention explicitly with your team member. It might sound like this:

> Hey Helen, look I do want to discuss that with you, but I'm just about to go to another meeting and I don't feel I'd be able to give you my full attention right now, I'm sorry. Would you be free at 4 pm to talk this through with me fully?

No-one ever says, 'Oh gosh no, I'd rather you just listen half-heartedly now please and then race off to your meeting before I'm done.'

By scheduling proper time for the discussion, the messages you're now sending are:

- you're important
- your issues are important
- I will make time for you, so I can fully listen, understand and support you.

I hope you've found this an interesting exploration of what we're listening for and how to overcome some common barriers to listening. After your chapter reflection, let's have a good look at the final element of our coaching approach: questioning.

DRA learning reflection

Discoveries:

- Being listening involves listening with our ears, eyes, heart and body.
- When we are deeply listening, we can hear more than just data. We can also listen for emotions, meaning and even the unsaid.
- Saying 'Yes but …' negates what your team member has said. Replace 'Yes, but …' with 'Yes, and …', even when you disagree with your team member.
- Interrupting your team member is a sign that you're not listening. Instead of listening, you're formulating and sharing your own thoughts.
- Confirmation bias wires your brain to listen out for what you already know.
- Assumptions cloud our listening and block out the intended message.

Reflection questions:

- On a scale of 1 to 10, with 1 low and 10 high, how would you rate your listening skills right now?
- What might your team members say about how you listen to them?
- Who listens to you really well? What do they do?
- When you're listening at your best, what's different about that situation?

- What are your most common barriers to listening?
- Who do you find it really difficult to listen to? Why?
- What's the key listening challenge for you?

Actions to choose from:

- When I'm listening to my team member, instead of just listening for the data and information, I will listen for their emotions and meaning.
- When I disagree with something my team member is saying, instead of saying 'Yes, but ...', I will say 'Yes, and ...' to acknowledge their contribution and then add my different opinion.
- When I'm listening to my team member, instead of just listening for what I want to hear, I will listen for things that challenge my perspective.

'The person who asks questions is more helpful than the person who offers advice.'

James Clear

Chapter 8

USING THE POWER OF QUESTIONING

When most people think of coaching, they only think of asking questions, and now you can see that there is so much more that comes *before* questions. You have taken the time to become present and this has unlocked your ability to tune into your team members with your listening skills. And now … *drum roll* … it's time to explore questions.

How you ask your questions is just as important as the questions you ask. Does the person you're asking feel like they are being cross-examined in the witness box, or do they feel you are coming from a place of genuine, non-judgemental curiosity? If you've really nailed your presence and your listening, I'm sure it's going to feel like the latter.

There are many interesting types of questions, and all questions are useful. The skill is using the right question at the right time. Let's start with the basics and build on.

OPEN AND CLOSED QUESTIONS

Here's a wee test.

Read the following questions. Can you identify which ones are open and which are closed?

- Do you know the difference between open and closed questions?
- How do you use open and closed questions in your daily work?
- What feedback have you received on how you use questions?
- Do people feel interrogated when you ask them questions?

Did you guess correctly which ones were which?

- Do you know the difference between open and closed questions? (Closed)
- How do you use open and closed questions in your daily work? (Open)
- What feedback have you received on how you use questions? (Open)
- Do people feel interrogated when you ask them questions? (Closed)

Maybe you know the difference already. Great! If so, this will be a useful refresher.

Closed questions

Closed questions are questions which can be answered with a 'yes' or a 'no'. Here are a few examples:

- **Are you** Scottish?
- **Have you** ever lived in Sydney?
- **Will you** be working remotely tomorrow?
- **Could you** join us for Friday's meeting?
- **Should you** have sent that email to our CEO?
- **Did you** see Max at his desk yesterday?
- **Can you** email me that report again please?
- **Would you** like to meet me for afternoon tea at 3 pm?

Closed questions support you to *close down* the conversation. They are very useful to wrap things up (like … 'Do you need any more support from me?') and check understanding ('Did you mean this … ?')

The one question in the closed question list above to be really careful with is the 'Should you … ?' question. I'll add a few more examples so you can get the picture:

- **Should you** have sent that email to our CEO?
- **Should you** ask James for his advice?
- **Should you** consider something else?

What is actually going on inside these 'Should you … ?' questions? Think back to your childhood; did you ever receive any of these 'Should you … ?' questions from your parents or carers?

- Should you really be up this late?
- Should you have eaten that last piece of cake?
- Should you have gone to that party when you have an exam the next day?

Starting to get the picture? They are framed as a question, but you can 'hear' the preference of the questioner in the question.

- Should you really be up this late? (You should NOT be up this late.)
- Should you have eaten that last piece of cake? (You should NOT have eaten the last piece of cake.)
- Should you have gone to that party when you have an exam the next day? (You should NOT have gone to the party.)
- Should you have sent that email to our CEO? (You should NOT have.)
- Should you ask James for his advice? (You SHOULD ask James.)
- Should you consider something else? (You SHOULD consider something else.)

Using 'Should you … ?' questions may also at times sound a little condescending, so just notice whether they are slipping from your lips and use them carefully. If you catch yourself doing this a lot (*and believe me, I've asked plenty of 'should you' questions in my time*) then jump into open questions and select another more powerful question instead.

Open questions

Open questions are questions that elicit an open-ended answer, meaning you don't know what answer you're going to get. Here are a few examples:

- **How** might we achieve that goal?
- **Why** do you think that happened?
- **What** are the best options to solve this problem?
- **Who** might be able to support you with this challenge?
- **When** are you going to do that?
- **Where** do you see yourself in 12 months?
- **Which** option do you prefer?

Open questions help you *open up* the conversation. They are very useful when you're having coaching conversations with your team members, particularly at the beginning when you're trying to get the conversation flowing.

Let's look at two open questions that deserve a special mention. 'And what else?' and 'Why?'

And what else?

When you've been talking with a team member and perhaps, they've come up with a few ideas and you add in 'And what else?' you encourage your team member to think more deeply and bring forward something additional to the discussion. In my experience, working in hundreds of coaching sessions, I've found that 'And what else?' uncovers amazing gems from the people I'm working with. The message you give to your team member when you ask, 'And what else?' is that you believe that they have more to offer; more ideas, more suggestions, more questions. Try it in your next conversation and see what happens.

Why?

'Why?' can have a bit of an edge. Sometimes it can sound, depending on your tone and emphasis, a bit accusatory. As in 'Why were you late?', which more often sounds like it has an exclamation mark at the end rather than a question mark!

In the workplace it might sound like:

- Why do you think that's the best option?
- Why did you take that course of action?
- Why would you like to participate in that program?
- Why do you say that?

'Why?' uncovers your team members' value judgements behind their actions – sometimes it helps to uncover a disconnect between their personal values and the values of the organisation, which you can then address. It can also help you understand how they came to take an action or make a decision; it takes you deeper into understanding the person. The most important thing to remember is to use it carefully and to use it with curiosity and an enquiring tone. You might even frame your question like this:

> I'm really curious to understand your decision making in that situation (frame). Why did you feel that was the best way to move forward? (question)

Engaging your curiosity when you use the 'Why?' question can make for really rich conversations. Just keep an eye on your tone.

Just notice your questions over the next few days. Are they more open or closed? Chances are they're more closed than you think. If you notice that you are using a lot of closed questions, just pick a new open question to try. You may consider sprinkling 'How?' liberally over your conversations and watch what happens.

Now that we have that clear, let's have a look at a question trap that can sometimes get us into trouble.

WHEN IS A QUESTION NOT A QUESTION? WHEN IT'S A QUEGGESTION!

You might not have heard of these before, but I'm pretty sure that a few of them may have made an appearance in some of your recent conversations. These sneaky little phrases *sound* like questions, but they are actually suggestions pretending to be questions! The term 'queggestions' was created by Michael Stratford, a US coach, and was introduced to me by my inspiring coaching mentor Em. Knowing about queggestions is a gift that keeps on giving. You may know them as leading questions, but I think Michael's label 'queggestion' is a cracker! Here are some examples:

- Do you think you should ask the CEO what she thinks about that before proceeding?
- Would our customers prefer the other option, do you think?
- That sounds like a big risk. Do you think we should proceed with that course of action?
- Do you think that's good enough?

Are you getting the picture? Really, they are just statements with a question mark at the end. The statements inside the above queggestions are:

- You **should** ask the CEO what she thinks about that before proceeding.
- Our customers **would** prefer the other option.
- You **should not** proceed with that risky course of action.
- I **don't think** that's good enough.

So, what if, as their leader, you have some concerns about where your team member is headed with a course of action – are you just supposed to let them blunder on? Hell, no! The good news is that there is a much better way of bringing an issue to their attention than using queggestions. Try using these open questions instead. The four queggestions above can be reframed as:

- What do you think our CEO might say about this?
- Which option would our customers prefer?

- What might be some of the risks associated with that course of action?
- How will you know you've been successful?

I know what you're thinking; 'Ah well, that sounds so easy Anna, but you don't know my team members! They are continually stepping on "land-mines" and I'm the one that has to clear up the mess! What if they just can't see the risks … ?' All good, my friend. Then all you need to do is share your opinion … as an *opinion*, not as a queggestion. The conversation between the leader and the team member may look a little like this:

L: Thanks for running me through your plan for this next project.

TM: No problem. I reckon we're good to go, right?

L: It's looking pretty good, yes. I just have one or two more questions before we finish up.

TM: Sure! Fire away!

L: What might be some of the other risks associated with this project?

TM: Hmmm. Well, to be honest I don't really see any other risks, apart from the basic ones we've already covered.

L: That's interesting. To be honest, from my experience I see that a little bit differently. I'm a bit concerned about the risk around … [and the leader goes on to share the details of their concern]

It's a lot cleaner. And you never know, the team member may have come up with lots of additional risks that you hadn't even thought of. It's important to give them the opportunity to answer the question. Then after that, you can add your opinion IF it's necessary.

SILENCE CAN BE GOLDEN

As you're learning to use fantastic questions as part of your coaching approach, sometimes you may fall into the trap of firing questions like a machine gun and the person you're working with feels like they're under attack! Instead of placing one exquisitely crafted question with your team member and letting them chew it over before responding, you hit them with two or three all at once and they sit there, bewildered, wondering which one to respond to first. Then, as they sit in bewilderment, you think maybe they misunderstood you so you fire out another question, and now they've got four questions on the table to deal with. This is not an effective strategy. So, what should you do instead?

...

Can you hear that?

...

Silence.

Asking a great question and then sitting in silence as your team member considers the question and then responds sounds really simple, but is in fact quite challenging. Why? It's because generally we find silence a bit awkward. As soon as silence falls on our conversations, we generally do our utmost to fill it and keep things flowing. But what if you allowed a little more silence in your conversations; what would happen then?

Silence can do the heavy lifting in conversations for you. A well-placed question followed by silence creates space for your team member to think. Space for them to reflect and consider their answer. Space for their opinion to form. Space to hear what they have to say, as opposed to simply having an echo chamber for our own views and opinions. Silence also infers that you believe they have something valuable to offer in response to your question.

How much silence is enough? When you're practising bringing more silence into your conversations, you can start by simply asking the question and then counting slowly from 1 to 10 in your head. I guarantee that by the time you have reached 10, your team member will have said something. Interestingly, counting to 10 also gives you something to do, to distract you from adding in your own thoughts too early.

If this sounds like a foreign concept to you, maybe like me you're a bit of a chatterbox, I'd suggest sharing with your team in advance that this is a new habit that you're going to be practising. I'll tell you a wee story to illustrate why this is important.

A few years ago, I was coaching a leader, let's call him Sam*. Sam had participated in a leadership development program and one of his key objectives following the program was to become a better coach to his team. He was as keen as mustard, and had bounced out of the development program back into the workplace, guns blazing, ready to become the 'super coach' he aspired to be. *Sounding great so far, isn't it?* As part of Sam's development program, he had three coaching sessions with me to support him in applying his learnings in the workplace.

On our first coaching call, Sam was taking me through his objectives and shared that he'd had meetings with each of his three team members already where he'd used his newly acquired questioning skills, but he sounded a bit perplexed about how things were going. I remember the conversation as follows:

Me: That's great to hear that you've been applying your questioning skills with your team Sam. Good on you for giving it a red hot go! I notice that you're sounding a bit perplexed; what's the challenge here for you?

Sam: Well, it's a bit weird really. I felt like I was doing such a great job of asking open questions and allowing silence afterwards, but my team was really upset after the sessions.

Me: Oh really? Why was that?

Sam: They all thought they were going to be made redundant!

Me: Oh wow! That's interesting. Why did they think they were going to be made redundant?

Sam: They told me that I was acting so weirdly, really different to my usual self, that they thought something was up and that they were going to be sacked!

I think Sam's team were thinking, 'Okay, so who are you? And what have you done with the real Sam?' Once Sam had shared with the team, after the sessions, that he was trying to implement his learnings and become a better coach they could all see the funny side, but at the time each team member had been very anxious about why their leader was acting so differently and what that might mean for them and their position.

Take a free learning from Sam's experience: when you're trying something new with your team, which might be using silence more to allow space for them, just give them a heads up about what you're doing. That will help in three ways:

- Your team won't get any nasty surprises.
- You demonstrate your openness to learning and trying new things.
- Your team can support you by giving you feedback on how you're going.

Questioning with curiosity is such an important skill for you as a leader. Questions are your most powerful tool to enable your team members to develop and grow, as well as resolve their day-to-day issues for themselves. As you move towards questioning and away from advice giving you will notice your team members becoming increasingly independent. Set yourself a challenge to ask at least three questions before leaping into advice, and watch the amazing results.

Chapter reflection ahead, and then we're off to part III.

DRA learning reflection

Discoveries:
- Closed questions, like 'Can you ... ?' and 'Do you ... ?', are really useful to wrap up conversations.
- Avoid 'Should you ... ?' at all times!
- Open questions, like 'How?' and 'What?', help you open up a conversation and get it flowing.
- Use 'And what else?' to encourage your team member to come up with even more ideas and deeper thinking.
- Be careful of your tone when you use 'Why?'
- Avoid queggestions – ask a question OR make a suggestion – don't run them both together.
- Let silence do the heavy lifting for you.

Reflection questions:
- On a scale of 1 to 10, with 1 low and 10 high, how would you currently rate your ability to ask useful questions?
- What might your team members say about your ability to ask useful questions?
- How might you improve your use of open and closed questions in your daily work?
- Who do you know that asks excellent questions? What do they do?
- What's the best question you've ever been asked? And why?
- What question would you really like to ask your team members? And why?

Actions to choose from:

- When I ask a question and my team member doesn't immediately respond, instead of firing out another question, I will count to 10 in my head and use silence before asking anything else.
- When I'm meeting with my team, instead of asking lots of closed questions, I will think of one or two really good open questions which will open up the discussion.
- When my team member quickly comes up with lots of ideas or responses to a question, instead of just moving ahead with their initial responses, I will ask 'And what else ... ?' to uncover more options.

'Are leaders born or made? This is a false dichotomy – leaders are neither born or made. Leaders *choose* to be leaders."

Stephen Covey

Part III

LEAD!

The lights have changed again. Green illuminates. You're ready to go. *Well, almost.* Time to start doing some people leadership things. But what things, exactly?

Now that you know how to learn, you've had a good look at yourself, your systems and your support crew, as well as engaged your coaching approach to leadership, you're ready to deliver on the five duties of leadership. Do you remember the story about Neve's first day and her exceptional leader, Steve? He knew precisely what those five duties of leadership were. Here's a brief summary to refresh your memory:

- He's genuinely interested in **connecting** with people.
- He's an excellent **communicator.**
- He can **focus** his team on what's important.
- He enjoys **developing** people.
- He supports his staff to **resolve any problems** they're facing.

Each of the five following chapters is going to cover one of these five important duties of leadership. We'll look at what they are and why they're important, as well as how to do them well. We'll also have a look at a few 'What if' scenarios you might face, and I'll share some ideas on how to deal with them.

The final piece in part III is a consolidation of your learnings into your very own people leadership development plan.

'Simply paying attention allows us to build an emotional connect. Lacking attention, empathy hasn't a chance.'

Daniel Goleman

Chapter 9

YOUR FIRST DUTY: CONNECTING WITH YOUR TEAM

BEGINNING

As you begin this chapter, where you'll learn how to connect well with your team members, you must first harness and apply all the learnings you've had on being present, listening and asking great questions in part II. They are the foundational elements of connection. Interestingly, while you will use these foundational elements consistently with your team members, the way you connect might look quite different depending on the team member concerned. (We're going to look closely at the differences over the next two chapters.)

'How so?' you ask.

I'm pretty confident you've heard the phrase 'Treat other people the way you would like to be treated', yes? From this moment on I'd like you to erase that phrase from your memory banks. Seriously, hit your internal <Delete> button. Replace it with the following phrase: 'Treat other people the way that THEY would like to be treated'.

Asking yourself 'How would I like to be treated?' and then treating everyone else the same is, I'd argue, a fairly selfish approach. News flash: not everyone is like you. It's good to remind ourselves of this, often.

Asking 'How would *they* like to be treated?' forces you to take a few moments to stand in their shoes and have a good look around through their eyes, and then consider your approach. This is empathy; the ability to understand and share the feelings of others. When your team members feel you really 'get them', you're demonstrating empathy and you are connecting.

How might you demonstrate empathy to your team members to connect with them more deeply?

Trotting out glib 'I know how you feel' cliches? Nope.

Listening to their stories and then adding in all the times when that happened to you? Nope.

Taking your team to an offsite and doing 'trust fall' exercises? Big nope. I really hope you're sitting there scratching your head thinking, *trust fall exercises? What the heck is she talking about? I've never heard of those.* In basic terms, a trust fall exercise is where you are blindfolded and your team stand behind you, you fall backwards and they are supposed to catch you and … abracadabra … that establishes trust. NOT. (Apparently no-one explained the catching part to my two kids many years ago when they played that game with my husband and he cracked his head on the bed frame – serves him right for doing a trust fall exercise I'd say! Poor Anthony.) Trust fall exercises aren't great for building connection, but they are great for evaluating leadership development consultants. If you're looking for some support for your team and a consultant mentions that they do trust fall exercises, just thank them for coming and delete them from your contact list. Job done.

When you demonstrate empathy and your team members feel like you get them, you will build connection, and as you establish connection you build trust. Connection is the precursor to trust, and – as you will already have learned through your own experience in the world – trust is the lifeblood of relationships. No trust. No relationship. Period.

While – as I mentioned – there isn't a one-size-fits-all magic recipe for connection, there are some important 'basics' you must get right to pave the way for success as you build your relationships and deepen your levels of trust with your team. You'll discover that you're never 'done' building trust; it's an ongoing, never-ending process. You'll also continue to learn about trust as you progress in your career. For now, though, as a new people leader, let's focus on helping you nail these basics.

THE MAGNIFICENT SEVEN

The seven components that follow are the trust basics and they are actually very simple, but disappointingly I still hear of many leaders who don't get these right. It would seem then that they're simple, but not that easy.

If you're already doing these things, that's great. They key here is *consistency*. You can't do these things sometimes; it must be almost always. Why 'almost always'? Because you're a human being and you're going to make mistakes, you're going to have 'off days' and slip ups, so 'almost always' is a good standard to be aiming for.

Let's get into it.

1. Start with an open mind

When you step into your first leader role you might encounter someone who just wants to give you a 'quiet heads up' about one of your team members. A friendly warning if you like. Hmmmm. Unless this person is your leader or someone from HR, be very wary about this. When you're building connection with your team you need to keep an open mind. The way you interact with each team member is going to be different from anyone else's experience because, as you'll learn more about in the next chapter, everyone is unique. When you listen to the 'quiet heads up' and form an opinion or judgement about one or more of your team members before you've even met them, you have already created a barrier to connection and will have activated your confirmation bias (which we looked at earlier).

When you meet with new team members, mine for gold. Look for what's good about them, what strengths they bring, how they might complement another team member's strengths. When you ask questions to find out about their skills, talents, wisdom and experience, you are more likely to connect. (Re-read the earlier pieces in the book about beliefs and growth mindset in chapter 2 if you need some extra help here.)

2. Hello and cheerio

When you come in to work at the beginning of your day, greet your team on your way in, or as they arrive. It might be a smile and a nod, it might be a cheery good morning, it could be a quick 'Hi, how are you today?' or a subtle wave to someone who's on the phone. Acknowledging your people is key. As a leader you set the tone for the team. I've had lots of program participants tell me over the years that 'my manager doesn't even say good morning to me'. How sad is that? Most of us have experienced this at some point. It literally takes less than one second (believe me, I timed it!) to say, 'Good morning'. Less than one second! In teams where the leader doesn't even say good morning, I'm surprised that anyone even bothers to show up.

What if you're working remotely? You might add a quick good morning to your group chat. Or if you have a five-minute check-in meeting at the beginning of the day, you can greet people there. Or you can say good morning on your first email or other form of digital contact for the day. The options are many and varied.

And when you greet them, if you are face to face (virtually or other-wise), notice them. Has one of your team dyed their hair pink (cool hair!), or is someone looking a bit sad (is everything okay?) or are they a bit pale (how are you feeling today?). Be present for your team. You're not a robot, and they're not either. Don't say good morning because you have to, say it because you want to. Say it to acknowledge them and make them feel welcome and valued – every day.

As with most things, there's a balance here. I'm not expecting you to jump up from your seat every time a team member arrives and rush over to their desk to greet them with a coffee and a muffin; you can simply say hi on your first interaction with them, or maybe mid-morning you just do a sweep around and say hi to anyone you haven't seen yet. You can do it on the way to the coffee machine or a meeting or even a bathroom break – again, plenty of opportunities to make this happen.

But beware – you can go too far:

I had a lovely program participant once who told me that his manager had to have a word with him because (with the best of intentions) he was shaking people's hands every single morning, and the team was getting a bit ticked off. Yep, that's a bit too much. Remember the Goldilocks principle – not too much, not too little, but just right. Just right for *your* team.

A similar approach can be used at the end of the day with farewells. Don't just disappear. Let your team know when you're heading home. Wishing your team a pleasant evening on your way out is yet another way to build connection.

Leadership tip: when your team work late

If you have a common finish or closing time with your team and someone seems to be working back, I'd recommend checking in with them on your way out to see why they're staying late. Encourage them to finish on time so they getting adequate rest, and if they're working back to meet a deadline, make a note to review priorities with them when you next meet so working back doesn't become a habit. Again, as a leader you set the tone; don't make working late a 'badge of honour' (which is all too common these days). Your mission is to take care of your team and ensure they are having appropriate rest.

3. Find common ground

What do you have in common? Were you both born in Melbourne? Did you both emigrate from Sri Lanka? Do you both listen to the same podcasts? Do you both have a passion for cycling? Do you both binge watch the same show on Netflix? If you ask enough questions, you will inevitably find something you have in common.

Common ground also helps establish connection. You can uncover common ground on social media: what do they like? What do they post about? Or you can just do it the old-fashioned way and have a conversation. A fabulous coach I worked with once always asks her new coachees, 'What brings you joy?' What an amazing array of insights that question can bring, and even if you don't share their joy of tap dancing or chainsaw sculpture or sashimi, you already know more about that person than you did before. Make it your mission to find some common ground – it can be a fun challenge for your whole team.

4. Remember

Do you remember what your team members tell you? Little snippets about their lives, their experiences, their values, their worries and their joys? It could be as simple as the names of the special people in their lives, it could be as complex as a challenge they faced in childhood. When you're listening, people tell you their stories. When you remember their stories, their highs and lows, you demonstrate that you care enough to retain those details because knowing them and connecting with them is important to you.

> I remember an executive in a company I worked in years ago who managed a very large department. He had an exceptional memory for family details. He could remember people's partner's names and their children, and would ask what they were up to. Family was an important value to this executive and he demonstrated this by remembering details about his team and extended team's families – this was how he built connection with others.

It's important to follow up on previous discussions. Your team member might have shared a concern, such as a child having trouble at school – ask what happened, and how are they feeling about that now? Or news about a special upcoming event – how did that go? Your team member might have shared a health challenge – how are things progressing? Looping back to your previous conversation to 'check in' and see how things are going will create deeper conversations for connection.

5. Say 'I'm sorry'

This one is a biggie! Admitting when you're wrong and taking responsibility for your mistakes when you make them is fundamental to trust and connection. Notice I say 'when' you make them, not 'if' you make them. You are going to stuff up from time to time, and if you don't, you're simply not trying hard enough. Mistakes are where learning happens, so I hope you make a lot. Unfortunately, there are some people in the workplace who lack humility and just won't own their mistakes. They look for others to blame, sweep things under the carpet, get defensive, deny what just happened or just avoid discussing the issue. Guess what? No-one trusts them.

When you make a mistake, own it. Immediately. And then get straight on to apologising and finding a solution to remedy the situation. Most importantly, learn from it. Endeavour not to make the same mistake again. When you continually make the same mistake and keep apologising but don't change your behaviour, your apology sounds empty and you will erode your credibility and trust.

6. Ask for help

You may be a little surprised to see this one in the list. Yet asking for help is an incredibly powerful way to build connection. Step back for a moment and think about how you feel when someone asks you for help. My thoughts and feelings when I'm asked for help are:

- This person believes I have something to offer them.
- This person values my knowledge, skills, experience.
- This person believes I have credibility.
- This person values my support.
- This person trusts me enough to share that they might be 'stuck' with something; they are being vulnerable with me.
- This person thinks that I am approachable and may be willing to support them.
- This person doesn't know everything; they are looking to learn from me.

Having read that list, let's turn this idea around. Imagine there was one thing you could do that would have your team members feeling and thinking that way. There is. When you ask your team members for help, look what messages you are sending them:

- I believe you have something to offer me.
- I value your knowledge, skills, experience.
- I believe you have credibility.
- I value your support.
- I trust you enough to share that I might be 'stuck' with something; I am being vulnerable with you.

- I think that you are approachable and would be willing to support me.
- I don't know everything; I am looking to learn from you.

Who knew that five little words – could you help me, please? – could have such an extraordinary affect.

Time for a story.

I was working with a CEO recently and he shared with me that he was having a few challenges with his team. The organisation was heading into a new planning period and the CEO had asked all his direct reports to undertake some preparation on their own about what they thought might be the most important priority for the business to focus on in the next period. When the team came together, several team members were well prepared and had some suggestions to offer, but a few responded that they had been 'too busy' to do any thinking and preparation on this issue and had nothing to share yet.

The CEO decided to give these team members the benefit of the doubt and granted further time for them to present their suggestions. The CEO also encouraged each of the team members to reach out directly to him for additional support if they needed it. At the following meeting, all but one team member was ready to present their reflections and suggestions. When this team member realised that he was the only person yet to fulfil the CEO's request, rather than graciously apologise and give a commitment to when he would deliver on this commitment, the 'odd one out' became defensive. He lashed out verbally during the discussion to such an extent that the CEO had to meet with him one on one after the meeting and advise that his behaviour was unacceptable. Once the team member realised his impact and stepped into a more constructive mindset, he asked, 'How were all the other team members able to complete this piece of work on time?' The CEO said simply 'they asked me for help'. What this team member (who also led a large team inside the business) had failed to realise was that his inability to ask for help was unintentionally sending messages about his own arrogance and fear, and was damaging his team's connection with their leader. This leader was also unintentionally sending the message to his direct reports that they had to figure things out for themselves when they faced a challenge, as asking for help is 'not what we do around here'.

Let's look at how arrogance and fear played out in this situation.

Arrogance:
- You (CEO) have nothing to offer me (team member).
- My current knowledge, skills and experience are sufficient.
- I have more credibility than you.
- I don't value your support.
- I know more than you; there is nothing I can learn from you.

Fear:
- I'm (team member) concerned that if I share with you (CEO) that I might be 'stuck' with something, bad things will happen.
- I'm worried about approaching you and concerned that you might not support me.

Arrogance and fear break connection. Asking for help demonstrates humility and a growth mindset. When you ask for help from your leader, your peers or your team members you create the opportunity to work together through a challenge, access their wisdom and demonstrate that you don't have all the answers. The vulnerability you're demonstrating through this process is fertile ground for connection.

7. Be polite

'Please', 'thank you', 'excuse me', 'you're welcome' and 'How are you?' Super simple. Super important.

A lovely lady I know, Rachel, brought her son to one of my son's birthday parties when he was small. As she dropped her son off, she crouched down in front of him and looked him square in the eyes and said, 'And remember you've got your manners right there in your pocket, so you can just pull them out whenever you need them, alright buddy?' Perfect parenting and perfect advice for everyone, really.

Manners cost you precisely nothing to use, they are permanently available to you, but when you don't use them the damage to connection is immeasurable. If you don't say please or thank you, you are being rude. No-one connects with someone who's rude. Get this one wrong at your peril. If you know someone who needs more help with their pleases and thank yous, refer them back to their parents.

How are you doing with the Magnificent Seven? Already nailing them? I hope so. If you are, you're off to a good start. If there's still work to do, no problem – now you know where to begin. Let's be clear: these basics will jump start your connection with your team members, and there's a whole lot more you can do (that's a whole other book!) once you get these basics down pat. Now, remember I said there's no 'magic recipe' for connection? There isn't. But now that we've talked about the basics there is a 'secret sauce' you should know about. If you want to be able to use the 'secret sauce' to build connection, we're going to have to talk about the 'C word'.

LET'S TALK ABOUT THE C WORD

Don't panic! I don't mean *that* 'C word'! The 'C word' I'm talking about is 'care'.

To lead into this exploration about why 'care' is the 'secret sauce' of connection we need to loop back to my conversation about manners. More specifically, the seemingly polite question, 'How are you?' I feel 'How are you?' requires a special mention for our Australian readers. Growing up in Scotland and then becoming an Australian-by-choice, I found the way Australians use 'How are you?' fascinating. It seemed to me it's used as a greeting, more than an actual question. I learned really quickly that when you hear the words 'How are you?' you don't *actually* tell the person how you're really feeling! If you do, you might notice a narrowing of their eyebrows and a bewildered look on their face as they breeze past you and realise you are still speaking as you respond to their rhetorical question. (I know, I'm being a bit cheeky here and exaggerating slightly for effect, but it is true, isn't it?) Both parties just say 'How are you?', neither person really answers, and then everyone just moves on. I guess it's a cultural norm.

How much 'care' sits inside a rhetorical 'How are you?' question? Not much. I'd give it one point for politeness and at the very least acknowledging the person, but that's about it. So, if that's not care, what is?

Care is so important I'm going to give you the dictionary definition:

Care

noun

the provision of what is necessary for the health, welfare, maintenance, and protection of someone or something.

serious attention or consideration applied to doing something correctly or to avoid damage or risk.

verb

feel concern or interest; attach importance to something.

look after and provide for the needs of.

Just read through that definition one more time. There are some meaty components in there. Providing for the 'health, welfare, maintenance and protection of someone' is a significant responsibility, isn't it? Did you know that with respect to the mental health of your team members the two most important people are the person's partner and you (their leader)? According to Michael Bunting, author of *The Mindful Leader*, a whopping 33% of a team member's mental health is attributable to their leader's behaviour. A third! That might feel quite daunting, but let's turn it around: you have a golden opportunity to positively impact your team members' mental health when you care for them. This doesn't mean that you need to become their counsellor – that's absolutely not your role. What I'm saying here is that by caring for your team members, having their backs, providing them with care and attention, demonstrating empathy, providing what is called a 'psychologically safe workplace', you can positively affect their wellbeing and build your connection with them. When you care for your team members you are looking after them and providing for their needs, and who wouldn't want to connect with a leader who does that?

Pleasingly, it seems that in some organisations a global pandemic has increased the care factor. As I write we are 19 months into the COVID-19 pandemic. I appreciate that tragically for many around the world this has meant the loss of loved ones, and for many also loss of their jobs due to the collapse of their companies. For those who have managed to pivot through the crisis or fortunately work in an industry unaffected, or even bolstered, by COVID-19, one of the benefits I've seen in organisations over this time has been the seemingly dramatic increase in the 'care factor' demonstrated by employers towards their employees, and by leaders towards their team members. COVID-19 has focused everyone on health and wellbeing; a common, unifying goal has been identified. Thankfully leaders seem to have moved past using 'How are you?' as a rhetorical greeting and now genuinely ask 'R U OK?', enquiring after the mental and physical wellbeing of their people. This is a change that I hope is here to stay.

How can you possibly connect with your team if you don't care about them? And if you honestly (and please be honest) don't care, now is the time to hang up your leadership boots and go do something else instead. Yes, unfortunately there are 'leaders' out there who don't care – I've seen them, you've seen them, and they are sadly far too common, but let's face it, they're not *real* leaders. Certainly not the kind of leader I'm encouraging you to be. For me, caring is a non-negotiable for connection.

Sharing is caring

When you care for someone, they need to be able to come to you and share their needs and concerns. It's also a two-way street: you need to be able to share your needs and concerns with them too. And you're the leader, so you have to show them the way. You must go first. When you share what's going on for you, sincerely and candidly, you open the door for your team members to do the same.

I'll give you an example.

I was running a workshop with a small leadership team. It was our first workshop together and I had previously met the CEO and one of the team members. The two other executives I was meeting for the first time at the workshop. The workshop was going well, and we'd got to know each other a little bit over the course of the morning. At lunchtime I was sitting next to one of the executives and she shared with me that her partner had a terminal illness and she needed to take a few phone calls with the team that provided his support services during the afternoon. I was very sad to hear of her partner's prognosis and amazed at the level of focus and energy this executive could bring to the workshop, while having such a heart-wrenching challenge at home. If she hadn't shared the situation with me, I would never have suspected a thing – she had her game face on. The fact that this executive would disclose this to me showed her vulnerability. I caught a glimpse into her larger world, outside work. I could connect with her more fully, not just as an executive at work but as the holistic human being she is.

When you care for your people, you allow them to remove their 'game face' and tell you what's really going on. This enables you to have empathy for their position and consider what else you might be able to do to support this person so they can feel and operate at their best.

This executive is not alone. Everyone, including you, has their challenges: mental or physical health, carer responsibilities, financial struggles, relationship breakdowns to name but a few. When you demonstrate that you're a real person – with your own challenges and concerns – just like everybody else, you open the door for your people to be candid with you in return, and when we see each other as we are, connection deepens.

WHAT IFS: COMMON CHALLENGES AND HOW TO OVERCOME THEM

First duty down, four more to go. You're really rolling now! In this first duty, you've learnt about the Magnificent Seven which will help you build trust and we've explored the secret sauce of connection: caring. Connection is a vast topic and perhaps you've still got some questions. Have a read through my answers below to some common 'what ifs' and see if that helps.

What if I've tried all these tactics and I still don't seem to be able to build a connection with one of my team members?

The best thing to do in this situation is arrange a catch up during working hours with this person one on one. Find an informal yet private setting so you can speak openly. Grabbing a coffee can be a good way to do it. Then:

1. Share your intention that you really want to build a strong professional relationship with them.
2. Ask them what a good connection with you would look like.
3. Ask them how they perceive your relationship right now.
4. Ask them what they think is the best way for the two of you to improve your connection.
5. Ask them if there's anything else you could be doing differently to improve your connection.

Approach the conversation with curiosity and see what you can discover. Remember, connection looks different with different people. Your mission is to find out what 'good connection' looks like to them.

What if our team has social events outside work hours where we build connection and one person doesn't join in?

There could be lots of reasons for this:

- Not everyone is comfortable in those settings. The extraverted members of your team might be, but maybe the more introverted or sensitive types find it a bit too overwhelming. (Check out Susan Cain's book *Quiet* for more insights on this issue.)
- Maybe your team member has a lot of commitments outside of work that prevent them from participating in these types of events.
- Maybe your team member has social anxiety.
- Maybe they just don't want to.
- Or there may be something else.

Again, tap back into your curiosity; just have a quiet conversation with them about how they are feeling. Maybe they are not concerned at all. Or maybe they are feeling excluded, because they are unable to join in. You can't mandate attendance at out-of-work activities, so think about how you might create an opportunity for some informal connection opportunities at work. It could be a simple question at the beginning of a team meeting:

- What's the most memorable holiday you've ever had?
- What's the number one thing on your 'bucket list'?
- If you were a famous film star, who would you be and why?

Or have an informal afternoon tea. There are lots of ways to have fun and build connection while you're at work. Ask each team member to put together their 'top three list' of activities they think the team could undertake to further build connection across the team. Then share their ideas with the whole team and get to work on the list!

What if a team member and I have started off on the wrong foot – how do I reconnect with them?

The first thing you need to do is 'call it'. It might sound something like this:

Leader: 'Hey Pascal, I'm sorry we got off on the wrong foot. I'd really like to be able to put a line under what's happened to this point and see if we can reset and move forward together. And I appreciate that there are likely things that both of us will have to do a bit differently. Would you be willing to give that a try?'

TM: 'Sure. That would be great.'

Leader: 'Great. I'm really pleased to hear that. Let's have a talk about what we need from each other and what each of us can do differently so we can improve. Would you like to go first?'

Then your team member shares what they think they could do differently and what they need from you, and then you return the favour.

Look for commonalities and lock them in as your 'ground rules'.

If they come up with something that you can't 'live with', you can use, 'That's really interesting. I see that really differently …' and then add in your point of view. And then work through the suggestions until you come to a landing. You don't have to finalise it in one session, just get the conversation started. Don't let things fester. Get onto it early and then it will be easier to get back on track.

What if I think my team member needs more support than I can provide?
You may already be doing an awesome job of caring for and supporting your team. During your discussions, you may find that one of your team members needs more support from you than you feel able or qualified to provide. This is often the case with team members who are suffering from mental health issues. In this situation, remember that you are not qualified to provide mental health support. You are not your team member's counsellor or psychologist, and you are not expected to provide that level of support. In this instance refer your team member gently to:

- your Employee Assistance Program
- their GP or specialist (if they have one)
- Lifeline, Australia's 24-hour crisis support hotline: 13 11 14
- other free or professional support services in your area.

Make sure you check back in to see how they are doing and whether there is any further workplace support they need from you.

Rightio! Into DRA learning reflection you go, and then I'll see you in chapter 10.

DRA learning reflection

Discoveries:

- Connection is the precursor to trust.
- There is no magic recipe for building connection, but there are some basics you must get right.
- Meet your team members with an open mind and 'mine for gold'. Look for what's good about them.
- Always greet and farewell your team members each day in a way that's appropriate for you and for them.
- Seek common ground with each of your team members. Ask curious questions.
- Remember what your team members tell you, so you can build your understanding and appreciation of them.
- Say 'I'm sorry' when you make a mistake. Own it. Solve it. And try not to make the same mistake twice.
- Ask your team members for help. Working through a challenge together is a great way to build connection.
- Use your manners.
- Care for your team members. Make sure they're okay. Refer them on, when they need more help than you are qualified or able to provide.
- Share your needs and concerns with them, and encourage them to do the same with you.

Reflection questions:

- What kind of energy do you create for the team each day? What else could you do to make it even more welcoming?
- How clear are you on the 'gold' that each of your team members brings to the team?
- How much does your team know about you? What else could you share with them?
- On a scale of 1 to 10, with 1 low and 10 high, how well connected do you feel with each of your team members? For those team members with whom you score lower, what else can you do to connect better with them?
- If you asked your team to tell you which of the Magnificent Seven you should focus on most to further improve your connection with them, what would they say?

Actions to choose from:

- When I start work for the day, instead of just quickly getting down to my tasks, I will greet the team in a way that works for them.
- When I make a mistake, instead of avoiding a discussion about it, I will acknowledge and own it with my team, apologise, and then ask for help to solve the problem quickly.
- When I'm talking with a team member and I notice that something doesn't seem quite right, instead of ignoring it, I will make time to be present with them and create an opportunity for them to raise any concerns or issues with me.

'Conversations are the golden threads that enable us to move toward and trust others.'

Judith E. Glaser

Chapter 10

YOUR SECOND DUTY: COMMUNICATING WITH YOUR TEAM

One of the most commonly occurring issues inside organisations is poor communication. Engagement surveys, cultural reviews, best employer questionnaires – whichever tool you choose to look at how an organisation is functioning, many of them come back with the same message: communication could be improved.

This organisational dysfunction occurs when there is a breakdown, or an absence, of effective communication between people. It's *not* an organisation problem, it's a people problem. And irrespective of whether poor communication is a challenge inside your organisation or not, communicating well with your team is an important duty for you as a people leader, because you are there to lead the way. Your role is to show people how good communication is achieved. This means you will need to devote quality time to ensuring that the communication flow between you and your team members is tip top.

The word 'communication' is used often, at home and at work, and is so broad as to be – at times – useless. To be honest, I do have an internal alarm system which is triggered whenever that word 'communication' leaves the lips of a participant in one of my programs. It's no sooner out of the participant's mouth than I've jumped right onto it and wrestled this beast of a word, 'communication', to the ground with my bare hands. Picture me on the ground with my hands firmly wrapped around communication's neck!

Okay, so that's a metaphor! What I *actually* do is I ask some or all of these questions:

- What exactly do you mean by 'communication'?
- How are you being when you're communicating well?
- How are you being when you're communicating poorly?
- If you were communicating well, what would I see you actually doing or not doing?
- If you were communicating poorly, what would I see you actually doing or not doing?

As I'm asking these questions I can hear the participant's thoughts: *Geez Louise, I really wish I'd never mentioned it!* It is a fascinating exercise though, to dig under the surface of this catch-all term 'communication' and see what it actually means.

UNDERSTANDING THIS DUTY

On our journey to deeply understanding this duty, we need to begin by understanding why it's important to know what communication actually means and then how we can do it well. I can illustrate what happens when we don't really 'get this' by using a personal example of a friend of mine (*another excerpt from The Book of What Not to Do!*). Let's call this friend Amy*.

At the time this story unfolded, Amy and I knew each other very well, having worked together for a time and then becoming fast friends. Amy and I had regular catch ups, often walking together in the early evening as we chatted through life's ups and downs, generally putting the world to rights.

What I noticed about our conversations was that one particular issue kept coming up over and over again. Amy would complain that her partner wasn't communicating. Amy was fairly forthright (some would say blunt), and would explain that she felt so frustrated as she had brought this to her partner's attention many, many times. 'I've told her over and over again,' she would say, 'she just needs to communicate more with me!'

This unfortunate crack in their relationship, like a scratch on a vinyl record (I'm showing my age here!) kept them stuck in an endless loop, unable to move forward.

No prizes for guessing what happened next – let's just say it wasn't a fairy tale ending. I wish I knew then what I know now and could have been of more assistance to my friend. Upon reflection, I wonder whether Amy's partner actually knew exactly what Amy meant when she said 'you're not communicating'. And even whether Amy could have broken down her needs into more detail. We will never know.

BUT the good news is that *you* can get this right from the start.

What is effective communication?

> Communication is the transfer of understanding from one person to another.

That's it.
Sound simple?
Simple, yes. Easy?
Well … sometimes it is, and sometimes it isn't. It depends.
As a people leader your duty here is to ensure that:

- you *understand* your people
- your people *understand* you
- you can support your team members to *understand* each other.

Why is this important?

It all comes back to the 'transfer of understanding'. As a leader you must feel confident that you understand not just what was *said*, but what was *meant* by your team members. I'm sure many of you have experienced that communication trap where someone uses a word or phrase and you think, *yep, got it, I know exactly what you mean*, only to find out shortly afterwards that they have a slightly different meaning associated with that word or phrase and you didn't 'got it' at all! It's a trap. I've said it before, and I'll say it again: when you assume things, it makes an ASS of U and ME!

The great news is that by harnessing your coaching approach you will have activated your ability to be present, to listen deeply and to question curiously, and these three abilities are the absolute core of exceptional communication.

So, what else is helpful when you're attempting to deliver on this duty?

I see two key elements. Firstly, ensure that you are flexing your communication style to meet the needs of each of your team members. Secondly, ensure that you are creating opportunities for communication to occur.

Let's break this down.

ONE TRICK PONIES VS ALL-ROUNDERS

I've got some bad news for you. There is no 'one best communication style'. You've probably observed leaders in your workplace and previous workplaces who are what I'd describe as 'one-trick-pony' leaders. One-trick-pony leaders have one way of communicating, and one way only. They use their preferred style of communication whether it's a match or not with the individuals in their team. And if you're one of the fortunate few team members who just happen to 'match' their style – BOOM! – you've hit the jackpot! Their style is really going to work for you. But if you're one of the unfortunates who're not a match – then it's not going to be much fun.

As a leader you need to be a communication 'all-rounder'.

Time for another story.

My son Miles is a keen cricketer and so, as is laid down in the rules of parenthood, I have become a Cricket Mum. (*It's not quite as glamorous as being a Dance Mum and your duties take a lot longer, but the scoring challenges are certainly preventing me from succumbing to early onset Alzheimer's! Ahem ... I digress.*)

Miles likes to think of himself as an 'all-rounder'. In the cricket world, when you say someone is an 'all-rounder' it means that they are equally good at batting and bowling, and that if you considered that person's skills on their own (either their batting or their bowling), either would be good enough to gain them a place in the team. And all-rounders have both. And they're at a standard where they help the team to win matches.

But wait for it ... there's more. This is my favourite bit:

A genuine all-rounder is quite rare and extremely valuable to a team, effectively operating as two players.

Let's say that again, 'an all-rounder ... operates as two players'.

So, what does this mean for your communication style? Well, it's a bit more complicated than cricket. There aren't just two options – batting and bowling – or two people you're dealing with. There are many, which is why you're going to have to flex your style. Not just in two ways, but in many ways.

Imagine if Miles was supposed to be batting and started bowling at the other batsman! That would be weird! Wrong choice for the situation. Similarly, if you have only one style and you use it with every single person you lead, some of the time it's not going to be effective. You won't be 'hitting sixes' with that strategy! You need to assess the situation and the person you're working with *and then* decide which communication style to pull out of your kit bag.

As Abraham Maslow, the renowned American psychologist, said:

I suppose it is tempting, if the only tool you have is a hammer,
to treat everything as if it were a nail.

Sadly, that's what one-trick-pony leaders do. They only have one style available, so they hammer every team member with the same style.

Now that we've got that straight (*phew!*) our work together is to transform you into one of these rare and extremely valuable gems: a communication all-rounder.

You might be thinking, *isn't this at odds with everything I've read about leaders being authentic though?* In a word: no. You're not changing who you are being at your core. You're not changing your values or your beliefs, you're changing how you communicate a message so that it connects with your team members. For me, leaders who lack authenticity feel slippery. You never really know what they stand for; they say one thing and then do the opposite. They don't walk their talk.

When I talk about becoming an 'all-rounder', what I'm saying is, have a good look at the person you're trying to connect and communicate with and adjust yourself to better move in step with them. The message can be the same no matter who you're communicating with, but the style of delivery will be different.

I run this really fun communication exercise in my leader development programs. Participants think of a project they're working on and craft a project update that they need to communicate to their team members or stakeholders. The project update is 'the message'. My team and I call this exercise the 'speed dating' exercise – we set the participants in rows facing each other, and in the first round they have to communicate the message in one style, then the bell rings, they change partners and then they have to communicate the message in a different style to their new partner. They do this activity four times. One message, four different styles of delivery. It's a real eye opener for them about how different the delivery can be, even though the message is exactly the same.

Sounds useful, hey? So, how exactly do you figure out how to adapt your delivery style to meet their communication needs? Let's get into it now.

FLEXING YOUR COMMUNICATION STYLE TO MEET INDIVIDUAL TEAM MEMBER NEEDS

In the consulting and coaching work I do with my corporate and coaching clients I use a range of tools and profiles to support development and learning. Inside my kitbag is one particular tool for communication that consistently gets five stars in terms of ease of use, practicality and personal insights. This tool is the humble DiSC Profile. I'm going to introduce you to this tool and the insights it offers over the course of this chapter, as it is the key to appreciating and executing how to treat others the way they would like to be treated and nailing your communication with them.

The research behind DiSC was initiated by an American psychologist, Dr William Marston. In a nutshell, DiSC is a situationally based, needs-driven behavioural tool. That's quite a mouthful! What this means is that in different situations you have different needs and therefore you display different behaviours to satisfy those needs. A super-simple example is when you're hungry (*your need is hunger*) you go and grab yourself something to eat (*your behaviour is: making some lunch, which satisfies your need*). Similarly in the workplace if you have a need for accuracy, you might double check your report or ask a colleague to proofread it for you. (*Need: accuracy. Behaviour: proofreading*)

DiSC has four predominant styles which we'll look at in a moment, and we each tend to have a preference for a particular style or style combination. That said, everyone is a blend of styles and each of us can, and will, demonstrate the four styles every single day. You can think of your *preferred style* as your 'default setting' or 'comfort zone'. To demonstrate that you can display all of the four styles, let me walk you through some workplace scenarios where you might find yourself using the different styles.

D style: dominance

It's planning time with your peers and your leader. Time to think about the year ahead and what you should be focusing on to support your organisation in delivering its results. Time to share what you see as the priorities for the next three, six and twelve months. When you're in this situation you're focused on achieving results and being objective about what this team might be able to achieve with the resources, skills, knowledge and budget you have available. You're very clear on where things need to head and have no problem sharing this with other people and ensuring that they're headed in the same direction. You're keen to get on with things – there's no point waiting around when you know where you're headed, right? Like an eagle, you're soaring way above the ground, with your eyes trained on your destination.

i style: influence

Now that you've set your key priorities for the next twelve months with your peers and your leader, it's time to get the team you lead on board for the journey. You talk with them about the big picture. You share how much you're looking forward to working together on this plan and see lots of exciting opportunities for the team as a whole and each team member. Your pace is pretty quick and you're leaping from idea to idea like a mountain goat scaling a cliff face. You're taking a high-level approach, and your focus is really on your team and energising them to move forward with you.

S style: steadiness

Now that you have your team broadly on board with the plan it's time to calm the pace and check in with each of your team members individually to see how they are feeling and what else you might be able to do to support them to be successful. Now you're focusing on their needs. You take into consideration how they tick. You take your time, step into their shoes, and like a loyal Labrador you show your support to them and make sure that they know you are willing to help.

C style: conscientiousness

Now that you're confident the team has what they need to start on the delivery of the plan and more detail about the plan has been created, one of your team members raises an issue about one of the projects they're working on. In this situation, you need to get into the nitty gritty. You need to get your teeth into the facts and evidence of the project and together with your team member figure out what is going on here. Your pace is more measured and methodical, and like a Jack Russell Terrier, you're tenacious and ensure no stone is unturned on your watch! You're working together to solve the problem and then come up with a solution for improvement.

Hopefully you can imagine yourself in each of those situations and see how your behaviour shifts to meet the needs of the situation. Now that you know that you *can* and *do* demonstrate each of the four styles every day, let's look more closely at the attributes of each of the styles – you might begin to find that you gravitate to one particular style more than others. This *might* be your preference style. (If you're interested in discovering your own DiSC profile and your preference, I've included more information for you in the 'Ready for a wee bit more?' section at the end of the book.)

To help you get your head around the basic style combinations, which will give you more self-awareness and more awareness of others, we'll use the following process set out in the diagram below:

- Step 1: Start in the centre oval below and follow your answers to see which style they lead to.
- Step 2: Are you more fast paced and outspoken (D or i) OR more cautious and reflective (S or C)?
- Step 3: Are you more questioning and sceptical (D or C) OR more accepting and warm (i or S)?

Find your (or somebody else's) DiSC style

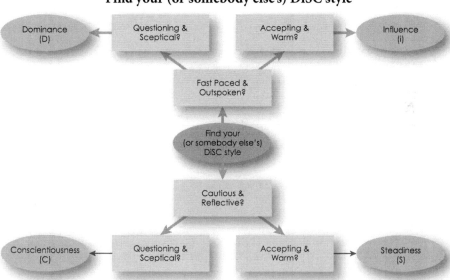

Now that you have a rough idea of your style (or somebody else's), have a look at the table of attributes that follows to see if this 'feels right'.

Now, there is a LOT more to the profile than this, but I feel at this stage this makes it nice and simple for you to get your head around and also consider

DiSC style attributes

Dominance (D)	Influence (i)
Key attributes:	*Key attributes:*
Priorities: Results oriented, taking action and challenging self and others	Priorities: Expressing enthusiasm, taking action, encouraging collaboration
Motivated by: Power and authority, competition, winning and success	Motivated by: Social recognition, group activities, friendly relationships
Fears: Loss of control, being taken advantage of, vulnerability	Fears: Social rejection, disapproval, loss of influence, being ignored
Observable behaviours: Self-confidence, directness, forcefulness, risk taking	Observable behaviours: Charm, enthusiasm, sociability, optimism, talkativeness
Possible limitations: Lack of concern for others, impatience, insensitivity which may result in collateral relationship damage	Possible limitations: Impulsiveness, disorganisation, lack of follow through due to a tendency to get distracted by shiny objects
Nutshell: Task focus + Fast pace	Nutshell: People focus + Fast pace
Conscientiousness (C)	**Steadiness (S)**
Key attributes:	*Key attributes:*
Priorities: Ensuring accuracy, maintaining stability, challenging assumptions	Priorities: Giving support, maintaining stability, enjoying collaboration
Motivated by: Opportunities to use expertise or gain knowledge, attention to quality	Motivated by: Stable environments, sincere appreciation, cooperation, opportunities to help
Fears: Criticism, slipshod methods, being wrong	Fears: Loss of stability, change, loss of harmony, offending others
Observable behaviours: Precision, analysis, scepticism, reserve, quiet	Observable behaviours: Patience, team player, calm approach, good listener, humility
Possible limitations: Overly critical due to perfectionistic tendencies and analysis paralysis	Possible limitations: Finds it hard to say 'no', tendency to avoid change, indecisive due to a tendency to please others
Nutshell: Task focus + Moderate pace	Nutshell: People focus + Moderate pace

how you might adapt your style to communicate more effectively with others.

For example, as an 'i' style my basics are People focus + Fast pace. I move pretty quickly, both physically and mentally. My friends would tell you that I talk fast and walk faster, and mentally I like to 'keep things moving' and like to bounce ideas around. I'm also very focused on people – I enjoy bringing energy to a group and inspiring people to be their best. I look for ways I can help people to be successful.

WHAT'S EACH TEAM MEMBER'S STYLE?

So now maybe you've got an idea of your preferred style, but what about your team members? Which style might they prefer?

Your team members might be the same style as you, or they may be totally the opposite – turn back to the 'Find your DiSC Style' diagram to see if you can uncover their style.

One thing that is very important to bear in mind is the 'situational' element of DiSC. In different situations our needs change, therefore our behaviours change. So, while you may not be able to identify someone else's *preference*, you can see how they're behaving in the situation you're in, so just go with that.

Challenges can arise when I'm working with someone who might have a totally different style preference to me, for example the C style (Task focus + Moderate pace), as they are completely opposite to my I style (People focus + Fast pace). What might I do here?

Well, I could dial down my pace, take things a little more slowly and methodically, and I could also dial up my task focus. Instead of being all about the people, I could think more factually about the task, or project, or program, and focus more on the data and information we have.

As for the person who has the C style preference, they could dial up their pace a bit more, maybe giving a higher-level view of things, rather than all the detail, enabling us to move along a bit quicker. They could also think more about the people and relationships involved in what we're discussing, rather than just sticking purely to the data and information.

Can you see what's happening here? Each person is attempting to flex their style to move more to the other person's style, and they will hopefully meet somewhere in the middle. The most important thing to remember when we're communicating with others is that all we can change is ourselves, we can't change the other person. There is no point having a tantrum in the corner and yelling 'why can't they just do it my way!' You need to meet them where they're at, and over time you will start to move backwards and forwards gracefully between the styles and establish highly effective communication patterns.

SOME TIPS FOR COMMUNICATING EFFECTIVELY WITH THE FOUR KEY STYLES

Now that we've walked through the four styles you might have better insight into your style and the styles of your team members. Maybe they're the same as you, maybe they're different. Opposite styles are complementary, so lucky you if you have some different styles to your own within your team. What's useful now is to consider how you might communicate *differently* with your team members given their styles. I've pulled together some great tips for each of the four styles which you can experiment with. Try some of the tips and see which ones help your messages land most effectively with your team members.

D style: Task focus + Fast pace
- Relate what you're talking about to the results you're/they're trying to achieve.
- Talk about the facts of the issue at hand.
- Talk about the big picture.
- Keep things moving, don't get bogged down in detail.
- Cut to the chase, don't bother them with small talk.

i style: People focus + Fast pace
- Relate what you're talking about to new and improved ideas and make it fun.
- Be enthusiastic about the topic.

- Focus on what you/they can do, rather than what you/they can't do.
- Focus on your relationship first, and the issue second.
- Ask for their ideas.

S style: People focus + Moderate pace

- Relate what you're talking about to the impact it will have on other people.
- Share your thoughts and feelings and ask for theirs, and keep them in the loop.
- Ask how you can help.
- Give them advance notice about what you're going to talk about.
- Identify ways you can collaborate.

C style: Task focus + Moderate pace

- Relate what you're talking about to how this will ensure accuracy.
- Share facts and evidence.
- Provide the detail which supports your opinion/suggestion/idea.
- Give them advance notice about what you're going to talk about, so they can prepare.
- Give them time to ask questions.

EFFECTIVELY FRAMING A CONVERSATION

Having looked at some unique tips to help us communicate with each style, I'd like to give you another technique you can use for ALL the styles. This technique is called 'framing', or 'signposting'. I mentioned this briefly in chapter eight. You may already be using this technique – it could be an unconscious competence – but once you know about it you can use it more deliberately and effectively.

The following phrases are all forms of framing:

- I have some bad news …
- This may be a crazy question …

- There's one thing I don't understand ...
- The reason I'd like to have this conversation is because I'm really focused on helping you be your best ...
- This might be a challenging conversation for both of us ...

That's not an exhaustive list – there are millions more. What do they have in common? They signal to the listener what's coming next, they provide a 'frame' inside which the conversation is going to take place. The frame provides context for them to listen in to. It's about focusing the listener on what to listen for. It helps prevent the listener being taken by surprise.

I have a wonderful CEO I work with, Brett, and we can have some really direct and frank conversations which we both really value. Sometimes when I feel what I'm about to say may be even more challenging or direct than normal I use this frame:

'Permission to speak freely?'

He always says 'yes'. (So far, anyway!) And it enables us to have really frank conversations, cut to the chase and resolve issues quickly and effectively.

TELL ME 'WHY?'

When you are communicating with your team members individually or your team as a whole, no matter what their style they all have one thing in common. If there is only one thing you take away from this chapter about communication, I would love it to be this: they all want to know 'why':

- Why do you think that's a good idea?
- Why are we changing direction?
- Why are we taking this approach?
- Why do you want me to stop doing this?
- Why did you think my report was good?

It is critical that you share with your team the 'why' behind each of your decisions and actions. When they know 'why', you provide them with the rationale for what's happening. They then have more information on which to base their own decisions in the future. When you don't discuss 'why' and they can't deduce the rationale themselves, they will continue to be reliant on you for decision making into the future. This makes them dependent on you and, as we discussed earlier, that is not an effective foundation on which to build your leadership.

CREATING OPPORTUNITIES TO COMMUNICATE WITH YOUR TEAM MEMBERS

Now that we've looked at how to flex your communication style to meet the needs of each of your team members, let's move on to see how you might ensure you are creating opportunities for communication to occur. When we talk about communication, we spend a lot of time talking about *how* to do it – we also need to think about *when* to do it.

One-on-one time

When you're leading your team, you need to make time to communicate with your people. Here's a phrase straight out of the Book of What Not to Do: 'my door is always open'. Personally, I shudder when I hear a leader utter that phrase. It *sounds* nice, but on whom does all the responsibility sit in that phrase? On the team member. If you use the phrase 'my door is always open', what I think you're saying is 'I'm available and you can come in whenever *you* choose', which is great, but you're not initiating communication with them. And that, for me, is where the problem lies. It places all the responsibility for communication on them. And if something goes wrong, or there's some miscommunication, it's the ultimate 'get out of jail free' card. 'Oh well, I don't know how that happened, I told them my door's always open … !'

You're the leader. You need to lead the communication and model how it's done well.

Set up a regular time and frequency for you and your team members to catch up. It's going to vary. For some people once a week for 30 minutes will be perfect. For others 30 minutes a fortnight might work, or some other timeframe. The most critical point here is that there needs to be a regularly occurring opportunity for the two of you to catch up.

The older I get the more I appreciate catching up with people one on one. It's not that I don't like discussing things in a group setting, it's just the communication is completely different. What I notice about group meetings is that:

- they can be dominated by the loudest voice in the group
- they can be a difficult forum for more introverted people to share their views
- not all of the topics discussed are relevant to all the people present
- due to the number of issues to be discussed, often discussions can be quite superficial.

When you communicate one on one with a team member, it's much more likely that you can:

- talk about what matters most to you and the team member you're meeting with
- hear exactly what they think and feel about an issue
- dig more deeply into an issue and come to a resolution
- clarify any issues or concerns.

When you are present with your team member in a one-on-one meeting, they will feel heard and the effective transfer of understanding between you both is more likely.

Have I convinced you that a regular one-on-one meeting with each team member is an essential part of how you lead? I hope so! One last point to nail this home: when you choose to spend time one on one with your team members (as opposed to using the 'my door is always open approach') you are implying 'I choose to spend time with you because communicating with you regularly is important to me'.

Team time

In addition to catching up with your team members one on one, it will also serve you well to have them meet as a whole team. Again, it's up to you, the tempo of your team and your organisation how often this is. Maybe it's monthly, maybe it's fortnightly, maybe it's weekly. Experiment with the frequency and find out what feels 'just right' for your team.

Catching up with your whole team is for discussion of 'whole of team' matters. It could be that you are providing a status update on the business to the team, or reviewing your results for the current period. You might also be discussing some common challenges across the team. The test for what gets discussed at this team meeting is, 'is this relevant for the team as a whole?' If it is, great! You can dig right into it. If it isn't, then you might need to set up a separate project- or issue-focused meeting separately that only has the relevant team members involved.

Your mission with your team meeting is to ensure that critical information is passed onto the team, to assist them to be even more effective and to seek feedback from the team on this information that you may need to feed back up the organisation. It's also an excellent forum for decision making. Think of your team meeting as a feedback loop and a decision-making forum. It's also an opportunity for your team members to ask questions, share ideas, challenge each other and work through things that are critically important to the team.

One trap I see is that some leaders fill their team meetings with 'interesting' presentations from other areas of the business. I'm not saying that presentations from other parts of the business aren't useful, but that's not what team meetings are for. Team meetings are meetings about the team, for the team. If someone has an interesting presentation you just *must* see, great! Make a separate meeting for that. Don't forsake the important work your team must do in team meetings for someone else's presentation.

Focus meetings

Perhaps there's a brand-new idea about something that impacts some of your team members, or something has 'gone pear shaped' with a particular project. Such issues are best addressed at a separate meeting. When we set up specific meetings for specific topics, we can really focus on that one thing, have a rich discussion, formulate some next steps and then get moving. Far better to have a greater number of shorter, focused meetings than a few longer rambling ones that keep falling down rabbit holes.

WHAT IFS: COMMON CHALLENGES AND HOW TO OVERCOME THEM

Wow! There's a lot to this communication business, isn't there? Hopefully I've distilled this significant duty down for you so you can really get to grips with it. Now that you have an idea of your style and the style of your team members and you've considered how you might adapt your communication so it really lands, let's have a look at a few more common challenges, particularly for those of you working virtually.

What if my team is virtual – what does this mean for our meetings?
I'm fortunate to have had experience with a range of both virtual and face-to-face teams. I've had face-to-face meetings when I worked in corporations and virtual ones when I worked as a consultant coach for an international coaching business. In my own consultancy with my team dispersed geographically, some near at hand and some far away, we use both virtual and face-to-face meetings.

If you're working virtually, you can use the same structure I outlined above, utilising video conferencing:

- one on ones
- team meetings
- focus meetings.

You can develop some rules of engagement with your team for your online meetings. Some suggestions I'd make are:

- Video ON for everyone (*When only some people have their video on, it feels like those with video off are spying on you, which is a very unpleasant feeling!*)
- Shut down other apps so you stay present to the meeting and are not distracted.

In addition, you might like to have some quick daily 'check ins' as you won't be running into your team in the corridor. This could be five minutes, just to see how they're doing and whether there's anything on their mind that they quickly want to discuss with you. Many teams use some kind of text service for this – such as WhatsApp, Google Chat, Microsoft Teams, or closed Facebook Groups – which can also work, so you don't necessarily need to use video conferencing. The most important thing to do is ask your team members:

- Which medium do you prefer?
- What would be the best way that we can communicate with each other?
- How regularly should we catch up?

What if my team has some people working virtually and some working in the office – what does this mean for our meetings?
Again, from my experience, I've seen three main meeting permutations and of course there may be many more:

1. everyone connecting individually
2. one or more remote people dialling in individually with one large group of people who are together in person
3. multiple in-person groups in different rooms connecting virtually.

If you possibly can, aim for the first permutation as it's far more effective. What I notice setups 2 and 3 have in common is that:

- one or more people can feel excluded from the conversation
- it can be hard to know who's speaking inside the large groups, for remote participants
- it can be difficult to read the body language of the people inside the large groups
- the large groups tend to start talking among themselves, rather than with everyone on the call, and it leads to a feeling of exclusion that makes it more and more difficult for the remote people to participate.

What I'd recommend in these situations is that where there is a mix, everyone connects individually into the virtual call, as in setup 1. It's either everyone face to face, or everyone individually virtual, but, as much as you can practically avoid it, not a mixture of both. Depending on your level of technology this may be challenging, but if this is how your team is going to be working in the medium to long term it is well worth the investment. When everyone is connected individually you can clearly see each participant, and everyone is involved in the conversations and there are no 'sidebar' conversations occurring which can seriously undermine your team dynamic.

What if I can't communicate the 'why' behind a decision to my team?

This happens. Perhaps it's confidential information or business sensitive or subject to legal action – the reasons could be many and varied. There are times when you're just not able or permitted to disclose the 'why' to your people. When this happens, I ask myself, 'What can I say?' Perhaps you could say something like this:

> I'd love to share the reason behind this decision with you, but unfortunately it's classified as 'business sensitive' information, so I'm unable to share it with you right now.

Most people will be able to appreciate the situation and your position and leave it at that. Basically, what I'm suggesting is that instead of telling them the full details of the 'why' behind the decision, you just tell them why you can't. This stops people guessing and feeling left out of the loop.

DRA learning reflection

Discoveries:

- Effective communication is the transfer of understanding from one person to another.
- One trick ponies are not effective communicators.
- When you're not communicating effectively with someone, adapt your style to better match theirs.
- Framing your conversations enables you to focus a team member's listening and prevent surprises.
- When communicating, whenever possible explain 'why'. When you can't, explain why not.
- Saying 'my door is always open' is not an effective communication strategy.
- Schedule regular one-on-one time with each of your team members.
- Hold regular team meetings and ensure that these are about the team.
- Have more, shorter, focused meetings and fewer long, rambling, unfocused meetings.
- When working virtually, have a short daily 'check in', to maintain connection in the team.

Reflection questions:

- On a scale of 1 to 10, with 1 'not at all' and 10 'regular, high-quality conversations', how well are you currently communicating with your team members?

- If you asked your team members about your communication practices, what would they say? Would they all say the same thing?
- How might you need to adjust your style to communicate even better with individual team members?
- If you could change one thing about your one-on-ones to make them even more valuable, what would you change?
- How useful are your team meetings? What might you do differently to make them even more effective?
- How relevant is your current team meeting content to ALL the team members?
- Which content currently discussed in your team meeting would be better discussed in separate focus meetings?

Actions to choose from:
- When I'm communicating with one of my team members, instead of automatically communicating in my own style, I will consider their style and adapt my style of delivery to match theirs.
- When I'm considering what to include in our team meeting, instead of just automatically adding everything to the agenda, I'll ask, 'Is this relevant to the whole team?' and where it isn't, I'll schedule a focused meeting.
- When my team is meeting virtually, instead of having some of the team face to face in a room and one or two people online, I'll ask everyone to join virtually.
- When I'm having challenging conversations, instead of just going directly to the issue, I will provide a frame so my team can anticipate what's coming next and why it's important.

'The difference between successful people and really successful people is that really successful people say no to almost everything.'
Warren Buffett

Chapter 11

YOUR THIRD DUTY: FOCUSING YOUR TEAM

SQUIRRELS!

My friend, Kirsty, who like me is really into personal development and growth, attended a conference recently. Kirsty is a family lawyer and she has a particular conference she likes to attend each year which has a range of speakers on different topics related to running a successful legal practice. I love hearing about her learnings when she returns, and often many of her learnings apply to my own business, even though mine isn't a legal practice.

One particular learning she shared with me, which resonated so much, was about squirrels. Yep, you read that right; squirrels! If you live in the US or the UK, you'll be very familiar with squirrels – sadly (for me) there are none in Australia. I love squirrels, particularly the red ones. They are cheeky little devils, bright eyed with their bushy tails, darting along the branches, searching here and there for food. As they run up and down the tree trunks, they call out to each other and then disappear into their dreys (homes) in the tree hollows.

So, what do squirrels have to do with focusing your team? Well, one of the speakers at Kirsty's conference was saying that new ideas are like squirrels. If you can imagine a scurry of squirrels (*Seriously! That's the collective noun … I kid you not! You're getting the picture now, right?*) on your desk, darting here and there, up, down, over and under, they'd be having a riot! There would be no way you're going to manage to get any work done. You're so busy trying to figure out just how many squirrels there are that you can't decide which one to grab first. Sound familiar?

So, what do you have to do? The speaker suggested 'caging your squirrels' and only letting three out at a time. That makes sense. If you're trying to corral squirrels, it's going to be much easier with three than a whole scurry. And I'd build on his idea to suggest that it might even be better to just have one. So, every time you have a new idea, you pop it in the 'cage', and then when you're deciding what to focus on you let one of the squirrels out at a time. Call me weird, but after Kirsty shared this story with me, I printed an A4 picture of a really fancy looking birdcage and placed it next to my desk. Every time I have a new idea, I write it on a sticky note and put it in the cage!

Expanding this idea a little, I'd like you to consider that whether it's ideas or priorities or objectives or key result areas or projects or something else, when you're focusing your team, they need to know what is most important.

UNDERSTANDING THIS DUTY

Moving on from the squirrel analogy, if you want to be able to put your hand on your heart and say with deep conviction 'I help my team to focus', you can see now that what you really need to do is get rid of the organisational noise, disruptions and distractions that can plague your team. When you and your team are prevented (consciously or unconsciously) from doing your best work, it breeds fatigue and frustration.

So how do you get rid of all the noise? As Warren Buffett asserts in the quote at the beginning of this chapter, you need to know what to say 'no' to. The only way you know what to say no to is to discover the few things that you are focusing on that are really important.

I was talking with a client the other day who was feeling so much pressure 'because we have so many shiny new projects that we have to complete and I can't get all of them done in the time I have, and I have no idea how on earth I'm supposed to even get to my "business as usual" work' (which were the duties set out in her position description). That's a lot of noise and unfortunately it creates a sense of overwhelm, which is all too common.

As a leader, your role is to prevent this overwhelm happening to your team members.

WHY IS FOCUSING YOUR TEAM IMPORTANT?

Ultimately you want your team members to be crystal clear on where they're going and why, and what matters and what doesn't. When they know this, they can work on what matters most and you empower them to make decisions. When they know where they are going and what they're focusing on it will be easy for them to decide whether a new opportunity that arises takes them closer to, or further away from, the direction you're headed. If it takes them closer, great! They'll take advantage of that new opportunity. If it doesn't, great! They'll know to say, 'Thank you, but no thank you'.

Think of it the other way around. When you don't know where you're going and why, and a new opportunity comes along, you think, 'Well it seems like a good idea, we should probably do it …' or you get stuck in the 'I don't really know' cycle of indecision. They are both bad options. Decision making is relational. The question is not 'is this a good opportunity?' per se, it's 'is this a good opportunity, in relation to achieving our purpose/completing this project/delivering on this outcome we've agreed on?'

Here's a really simple example:

One of your team members is in charge of stationery supplies and equipment for the team. They notice that a lot of paper products with your usual supplier are heavily discounted and they think that purchasing them will save money, so they go ahead and purchase the supplies.

Sounds like a good idea, right? Getting a discount and saving money; yes, at first glance it does.

But what if the goal of the organisation overall was to go paperless? Then buying cheap paper supplies wouldn't make any sense at all. The opportunity in and of itself is a good one, but *in relation to* the objective of going paperless, it isn't.

Your team members need to understand why their team is here and what the team is focused on so that they can make better decisions *in relation to* this knowledge, and when they do that, your team will gain momentum and move forward more effectively.

When your team members are unfocused, they become unable or unwilling to make effective decisions, and so what happens? All the decisions fall back on you. And when that happens, you're really going to find out what being overwhelmed feels like! As Dan and Chip Heath say in their excellent book on managing change and transition, *Switch*, 'What looks like resistance is often lack of clarity'. When your team seem unfocused or resistant to moving forward, check how clear they are on what they're supposed to be focused on.

Let's now zero in on how you might go about focusing your team.

HOW DO YOU FOCUS YOUR TEAM?

The COVID-19 pandemic has been an excellent teacher on how to focus your team. In fact, it has even taught us how to focus organisations. During the pandemic what I noticed was that it became very clear, very quickly, what was most important for organisations.

COVID-19 became a unifying force for leaders as they focused on taking care of the people in their charge and adjusting how they did business. Many people have spoken to me about how their team has felt more connected and more focused since COVID-19 emerged. How did COVID-19 do this? It stripped back all the non-essential 'priorities' inside organisations, leaving only one or two things that mattered most. I place 'priorities' in quotation marks as this is often where leaders go wrong.

In many cases when I ask leaders what they're focused on right now, they provide a long list of items. How long the list is depends on where that leader is positioned inside the organisation. Generally speaking, the closer the leader is to the senior leadership team, the longer the list! But when you've got 47 priorities, where do you even start? Instead of providing laser focus for your team, you scatter them far and wide as each team member sets off on a mission to achieve one or many of these elusive priorities. Focus is diluted and cohesion erodes.

If you picture in your mind's eye how you can use a piece of glass like a lens to focus sunlight on one spot to create a fire, I want you to imagine that you are the lens. And when you focus your team's attention on one spot, believe me, you will start a fire! Their results will burn brightly.

When your team members know what is important, by default they also know what is NOT important and they become empowered to start saying 'no' to things that are not on the important list. This enables the team to build momentum, reduce distractions and ultimately get sh*t done.

As a new leader there are three particular questions to focus on. These questions, which I believe you need to be able to answer to focus your team, come from Patrick Lencioni's book *The Advantage: Why organizational health trumps everything else in business*. They are:

1. Why does our team exist?
2. What's always important?
3. What's most important for our team, right now?

Let's look at each of the questions in turn and see how you might focus your team.

WHY DOES YOUR TEAM EXIST?

I can't tell you the number of times I've asked clients this question and they struggle to answer it. A few months ago, I was working with a corporate services team and the leader of that team confessed that she was really struggling to articulate the reason for the team's existence succinctly, even though she's been leading them for years. She was clear about what they do, but articulating 'why they do' seemed a little elusive.

So, if you're struggling to clearly define why your team exists, know that you're not alone. It can be a very tricky question to answer well.

Bear in mind that why you exist is not about 'making money'. Money is an outcome or a result. It's certainly not what makes most people bounce out of bed in the morning, eager to get to work – unless you're a banker or a broker, of course, where your job *is* to make money for other people!

Team discovery: why are you here?

Maybe you're fortunate and you really know your team's 'why' already. If you don't, here's what you can do:

1. Ask your team to consider, individually, why your team exists. No sharing at this stage! If your team are deep thinkers, you may like to give them this question ahead of time, so they have plenty of time to think about it before you come together. What's important at this stage is to get lots of slightly different ideas and make sure every person has an opportunity to contribute.

2. When they're ready, ask each of them to write down a short sentence or phrase that captures this reason. Not a huge rambling paragraph, not 16 dot points, just one succinct sentence.

3. Then ask each team member to share their short phrase, and capture all the individual sentences and display them together; you could use a flip chart or a digital whiteboard – anything that allows the team to look at all the sentences together at the same time. Often people write down what the team *does*, rather than *why* the team exists, so as you review the sentences ask, 'Is this a what or a why?', and keep checking in with the team.

4. Look for commonalities and differences. What are we all in agreement about? Who has something a little bit different that seems to capture the essence of the team perfectly? Then consolidate the team's contributions into the best possible description of why the team exists. We're aiming for a single sentence, a concise 'one liner', that everyone can live with. When you do this well, it's synergy in action. The resulting single sentence is even better than any of the individual contributions.

If the team is struggling with the 'Why does your team exist?' question, you could also prompt their thinking with the following questions:

- What unique value does our team bring to the organisation, and why is that important?
- If we sat in the shoes of our stakeholders/internal clients/colleagues, why would they say we exist?
- What would be missing if we weren't here and why is that important?

This 'why' needs to be BIG! When you think you've got your 'why', try to go a little bit deeper. You're trying to find the absolute deepest reason. You can use the 'Five Whys' technique, which is when you attempt to ask Why five times – channel your inner three-year-old – to make sure you've got as deep as you can. When I ran this exercise with my consulting business we landed on:

We exist to inspire people and enable them to flourish

Everything we do is about that, and if an opportunity comes along that isn't about inspiring people and enabling them to flourish then we don't do that thing.

Similarly, when your team is really clear on why they are here then they too can support you to evaluate opportunities as they come along – are they a match or not a match? Now everyone is clear on why you're here and how you can best fulfil your purpose.

Now that you've got the big why clear, we can dig in a little more to the detail. Let's have a look at which things are always important to your team.

WHAT'S ALWAYS IMPORTANT?

In any team there will be some core elements that are always important. These are the things that 'keep the lights on' in your team, so to speak. They are the things that your team must *always* pay attention to and that are always expected to be delivered from your team. Here are some examples to get you thinking:

- for a call centre team: call quality, net promoter score, complaint resolution
- for a construction team: safety, project budget, project pipeline
- for a cafe team: customer experience, marketing, hygiene
- for a finance team: compliance, reporting, customer service.

Again, maybe you're really clear on what these things are ... but maybe you aren't. Even if you feel clear, it's fascinating to see what your team would say.

Team discovery: what's always important?

Here's an exercise you can run, similar to the previous one, to determine (or reaffirm) what your team must always be paying attention to:

1. Ask your team to consider, individually, what your team does that is *always* important. They are the things that you just simply cannot afford not to do. Again, no sharing at this stage! We want everyone to think about this on their own as we want to make sure we flush out every possible element that could be on this list. Ask them to write down their ideas – that way they are more likely to share them all with you.
2. When they're ready, ask each team member to share their suggestions and write up all the points somewhere everyone can see them. Where team members come up with the same suggestions, instead of writing the same thing multiple times, just give that particular item a tick to indicate that more than one person has suggested it. Some words may end up with multiple ticks if they are suggested by every team member.
3. You'll now notice the themes: those items that many team members suggested in common.
4. What about the differences? Are some things worded differently, but essentially they mean the same thing? If so, massage the wording so that everyone can 'live with it'. Where there is a disagreement, just ask, 'Is this something that we have to focus on ALL the time?' If so, it's in. If not, it's out.
5. By now you should have a list of the elements that your team always needs to focus on.

By completing this exercise you've now figured out what your team continually needs to pay attention to, to ensure that your team is delivering on its key purpose.

WHAT'S MOST IMPORTANT FOR THIS TEAM, RIGHT NOW?

In addition to the key elements that your team is focused on that enable you to deliver on your purpose, there may be some short-term issues that matter 'right now' and that need your team's attention. Here are some examples below:

- For a call centre team: maybe some legislation has changed and you have to train your consultants on what they need to do differently on the calls so that you can fulfil your legal obligations.
- For a construction team: maybe you've just had an accident on site and you realise that safety needs some extra attention right now.
- For a cafe team: maybe you've just refurbished your cafe and you'd like to attract a slightly different type of customer, and this is going to require a different angle to your advertising.
- For a finance team: maybe you've got an audit coming up in a few months' time and you need everything ready so you can pass with flying colours.

What you'll notice is that there is a specific challenge or opportunity within these examples and a specific outcome that needs to be met:

- For the call centre team: legislative changes implemented.
- For the construction team: safety improvements implemented.
- For the cafe team: new customers attracted.
- For the finance team: audit successfully completed.

These items have a 'due date' if you like. A time, in the short term, by which they must be completed. When your team has achieved these objectives, they may move onto something else, or simply maintain their focus on the key elements in the previous section.

Creating clarity around your team's 'why' and knowing what you need to regularly pay attention to, to keep 'business as usual' working well, is vital. When you combine this with a current priority – what matters most right now – your team will be clear on how to effectively prioritise their activities, what to say 'no' to, and how best to use the resources inside your team to get the best possible result for your organisation.

WHAT IFS: COMMON CHALLENGES AND HOW TO OVERCOME THEM

What if there are so many 'right nows' that the core elements are unable to be delivered and the team starts to divert from delivering on its core purpose and team members are becoming overwhelmed?

Your role here is to understand the capacity of your team. How much time does your team collectively have available? When you take into account the time needed to deliver on your key responsibilities, how much time is left for other projects or challenges? If the additional focus area is going to take up all the remaining time then you won't be able to take on any more projects or issues until that one is completed. If you are feeling pressured to take on something more when you know the capacity isn't there, you might like to consider the following phrases:

> I'd love to support you with that, but my team is currently at capacity – we would be able to help you with that project from [insert date].

Or perhaps the following question, which is particularly useful for your leader or people higher than you in the organisational pecking order:

> I'd love to support you with that, but my team is currently at capacity. What would you like us to stop doing so that we could take that on?

What if my team and I are not clear what we should be focusing on?
This happens. If you've tried the activities in this chapter and still feel a bit fuzzy on what you should be focusing on, I would recommend raising this with your manager. In addition, you can also visit your key customers – they could be internal or external – and ask them to share with you two things:

1. What are the services/products/processes you most value from our team?
2. What are the top three things you would like our team to deliver on this year?

Once you've spoken with a good range of your customers you will start noticing the commonalities or themes in question one and you can use this feedback to create your 'always important' list.

Secondly, from question two you will have a few short-term priorities that you can start to focus on and schedule, so that your customers get what they need from you and your team.

What if there is just too much on my team's plate?

You might have worked through this chapter and discovered some of the reasons why your team is overwhelmed. Unclear priorities perhaps, and the corresponding saying 'yes' to things you should be saying 'no' to. If you've got to this point and you still feel there is too much on your plate, it's time to have a courageous conversation with your leader.

When you can show that you're really clear on why the team exists, you're clear about what is always important for the team to deliver on, and you're clear on current projects and the team's overall capacity, and perhaps you've even received feedback from your key customers about what they really need from you, then you're in a much stronger position to articulate where the problem is and suggest what might need to be 'paused for now' until you make headway with the issues that are actually at the top of the list. Approaching your leader with a potential solution (and not just the problem you're trying to solve) will be received much more constructively and demonstrates that you've done your homework. And if your leader insists that everything needs to be done, you might like to discuss recruiting additional resources to supplement the existing team's capacity.

DRA learning reflection

Discoveries:

- Focusing your team prevents them from becoming overwhelmed.
- Multiple priorities dilute focus and erode cohesion.
- Knowing why your team exists enables you to establish what's important and what matters most.
- Knowing your team 'why' helps you decide what to do and what not to do.
- Knowing what's always important for your team helps you understand what you need to do to deliver on your why.
- Having a clear and single priority, instead of multiple, competing priorities, enables your team to come together and deliver on specific challenges.

Reflection questions:

- On a scale of 1 to 10, with 1 low and 10 high, to what extent are you clear on why your team exists?
- If you asked your team members, why would they say your team exists? Would they say the same thing?
- What are you and your team currently working on that does not contribute to delivering on the team's purpose?
- What are you not currently working on that would?
- What might you need to change to ensure you are delivering on the elements that relate specifically to your purpose?
- How clear are you on your team's number one priority right now?

Actions to choose from:

- When I'm allocating activities to my team members, instead of just handing them over, I will explain how each of the activities relates to achieving the team why.
- When I feel that my team members are resisting taking on a task or activity, instead of just pushing harder, I will ask questions to understand what they're unclear about.
- When I'm asked to take on a new project or task, instead of automatically agreeing, I will determine whether it connects with our purpose and priority and then accept or reject accordingly.

'Each of you is perfect the way you are ... and you can use a little improvement.'

Shunryu Suzuki

Chapter 12

YOUR FOURTH DUTY: DEVELOPING YOUR TEAM

Can I share a secret with you? While I love all the duties of leadership, I think this one would have to be my personal favourite. Inspiring and enabling people to flourish is the reason I jump out of bed every morning. It makes me feel excited to come to work, and I hope my passion for development flows into my home life too, enabling me to inspire my family and friends to be their very best as well.

For me, there is no finer feeling than watching someone take that first, tentative step forward. They may doubt their abilities, but with encouragement they 'have a go', they have a small win and their self-assurance grows. Inside I feel a warm glow as I watch them rise.

And sometimes, inevitably, on that first try they fall. (No, it's not a typo! I mean 'fall', not 'fail'!) Simon Sinek encourages us to use the language of falling not failing. Our team members fall down, they trip up, they stumble, things don't go quite the way they planned. It's not terminal, it's not failure. It's learning. We need to encourage and support them to stand up again, regroup and keep trying.

Either way, whether your team members have a small win or a small fall, they LEARN! Let's have a look at what it means to develop your team.

UNDERSTANDING THIS DUTY

To truly deliver on this duty of developing your team we have to start by understanding the distinction between training and development. Like the words 'manager' and 'leader', 'training' and 'development' are often used interchangeably. But they shouldn't be. (Full disclosure here, during my career, prior to starting my own business, I spent 12 years in corporate training and development roles, so I can get a bit tetchy when these words get mixed up!)

Let's have a closer look …

Training

Training is important. It relates to the specific knowledge, skills and competencies that your team members need to perform effectively in their roles. Here are some examples to help you get your head around training:

- If you lead a team in a call centre then your team members may undertake training in how to navigate the call queueing system so that they can manage inbound calls. They may also be trained in how to deal with angry customers.
- If you lead in a construction team then your team members may undertake training on how to operate particular pieces of equipment, like an excavator or a bobcat. They may also be trained in how to undertake a hazard and risk assessment for the work they are about to perform, to keep themselves and their teammates safe.
- If you lead in a cafe then your team members may undertake barista training so that they can make that perfect cup of coffee for this morning's caffeine-deprived customers. They may also be trained on the point-of-sale system, so they can operate the till.
- If you lead a finance team then your team members may undertake training in your company's accounting software, or auditing processes.

If there is an everyday activity related to one of your team member's roles that they are as yet unable to perform, it's likely that what they need is 'training' to address this need.

Training takes lots of different forms. It could be a formal course. It could be having a fellow team member (or yourself as their leader) show them what to do. Or they might just watch a video or follow a step-by-step guide. As a leader it's important that you understand your team's training needs and support each team member to fulfil them.

More on how to do that a bit later. But for now, let's move on to development. How is development different from training?

Development

Sadly, I feel that development is often the poor cousin to training. In fact, I note it's more like the second cousin twice-removed. (*I mean, that's a really, really, poor cousin, right?*)

Training is focused on the everyday, on the job, on skill levels; its focus is the role the person is *currently* in, whereas development is much more focused on the person's potential for growth and their *future* aspirations. So, when you're developing your team, rather than tying back specifically to the job they are currently in, you're very much looking at the potential each person has and projecting forward to see how you might enable them to become all that they can be. Development is very holistic.

Wow! That sounds BIG, right?

Feeling daunted?

Good. You should be! This is IMPORTANT!

Let's just reinforce the key message here: sending one of your team members off to 'tick the box' on a mandatory annual refresher for a Work Health & Safety program is NOT development. It's training. As I've said, training is very important and it needs to be done, but you need to be clear that it's NOT development. As a leader, it's your duty to support your team members to learn and grow, to develop them *as people*. When you develop your team, you are investing in their future. This is a huge responsibility and not to be taken lightly.

Let's have a look at a few examples to help consolidate your understanding of what development is:

- Iluka is currently working as a team expert in a call centre, supporting team members to create an excellent customer experience. Iluka is keen to make the move from his current expert role to team manager, where he would lead the team directly. Development activities for Iluka might involve shadowing a team manager to understand the role and observe the new behaviours he might need to adopt. Or Iluka might act in a team manager position to cover for an existing team manager while they are on leave to build his experience in the role. Iluka may also seek out a mentor who has already made the transition from expert to team manager and can now support him to make this move.

- Lucy is currently working as a labourer in a construction team. Lucy doesn't currently hold any formal qualifications and wants to undertake some development so that she has some broader career choices down the track, particularly given the physical demands of her current role. Lucy is considering developing her project management abilities. Development activities for Lucy might involve undertaking a literacy program to improve her reading and writing skills so that she can undertake further study. Lucy might also participate in a TAFE program to start the process of recognising and translating her hands-on work experience into a qualification.

- Heather is currently a barista in a thriving local cafe. One day she hopes to open a cafe of her own. Heather's development may be stepping into the floor manager's shoes when they are on leave to get some experience running the cafe's operations or she may undertake a small business start-up program.

- Kirra works in the accounts payable team inside a large organisation. Kirra is fascinated by systems and technology and would like to develop her career towards IT. Kirra's development may involve participating in an upcoming financial systems upgrade project to build her understanding of IT and create some networking opportunities with people in the IT teams, so that she can gain insight into what it means to work in IT and what skills and behaviours she might need to develop if she wishes to pursue a career in IT.

Development goals

When you look at the examples above you can see some examples of what development activities might look like. Let's draw out the development goals as it's really important that you understand the difference between development goals and training needs so that you can ensure your team members receive both. Let's use the four examples above to draw the distinction:

Team member	Training needs	Development goal
Iluka (call centre)	• Call escalation process • Quality assurance process	• Become a team manager
Lucy (construction)	• Construction white card • Scaffolding licence	• Become a project manager
Heather (hospitality)	• Latte art training • Food handling practices	• Open her own small business (cafe)
Kirra (finance)	• Advanced Excel program • Xero accounting software training	• Transition her career to IT

So, there we have it. You can see now how training is very current-role centred and very much about the here and now, whereas development is person-centred and looking to the future. Both are important.

In my experience I see some attention by leaders to training their team members, although it can be very inconsistent, but precious little time is spent focusing on development and that's a major problem. Let me share why development is also important.

Why is developing your team important?

Think about why undertaking development is important for *you*. What would you say?

Here's what I came up with:

1. It's fun.
2. It's challenging.
3. It's stimulating.
4. It helps me improve what I'm doing.
5. I get to meet new 'teachers'.
6. I get to learn new things.
6. I get to hear alternative perspectives and opinions.
7. It helps me re-evaluate what I'm doing and consider whether I might do it differently into the future.

8. It builds options for my future; it opens my mind to different possibilities.
9. It allows me to have more variety in my work.
10. It helps me fulfil my potential.
11. It helps me achieve my goals.

If I had to summarise that list, I'd say development engages me, enables me to become my best and makes me feel good.

Let's flip this back to your team now. When your team members understand that you are supporting them to become their best, how do you think they are going to feel about you as their leader? I'd say they will love your leadership and be sticking to you like glue! The fancy words for this are *engagement* (how connected your people are to you, your team and your organisation) and *retention* (how likely your team members are to stay with you). So, when you develop your people and build their ability to contribute to your team and your organisation you increase their engagement AND you will retain them for longer. These are two pretty compelling reasons, aren't they?

But wait! I often hear people say, 'If I develop my people they *may* leave!' *Newsflash*! I can absolutely guarantee you one thing: if you *don't* develop your people, they definitely *will* leave!

Let's turn this around. If *you* were in *their* shoes and you had a leader who was not interested in what you want to be when you grow up (*and as I write this book, I'm 48 and I love what I do and yet I still wonder what I'm going to become when I grow up, so I'm not being facetious when I write that phrase!*) and invested no time in understanding your desires and aspirations – are they the kind of leader you want to work with? Here are two little stories, to help build your confidence that developing your people is not going to cause them to leave.

I remember the day I started in the role of Training & Development Officer at Snowy Hydro. It was to be the first of many roles I undertook with this iconic Australian hydroelectricity company. I had my first meeting with my new manager, Shane.

Shane said to me, 'We're going to turn you into a $100,000 manager.'

While at that time, back in 2001, the money aspect may have been quite enticing, what really jumped out to me in that statement was the 'turn you into' component. That's development! They're keen to develop me! Woop! You have my full attention! Sign me up! It's my first day and they are already thinking of my future. This comment, and other initial experiences with Shane, created huge excitement for me as I joined this new company. I really wanted to work for THIS leader. This leader wanted to support me to learn and grow.

Another example comes from my husband, who is a General Manager within a NSW public service agency. The NSW public service has a very comprehensive secondment program. The program allows employees to move into different roles temporarily and gain new knowledge, skills and experience. With a program like this there's always a risk that team members who go on secondment do not return. How does Anthony combat this?

Anthony is a very developmentally focused leader; he believes in his people and their capacity to learn and grow. As his team members move into and through their secondments, they return with their newfound skills and experience to advance through Anthony's organisation. If Anthony took the 'if I develop them, they'll leave' approach then he wouldn't approve their secondments – and people would resign to gain this additional experience. By taking a broader developmental approach Anthony retains great people in his organisation who are continually learning and growing (through their secondment experiences) and bringing their new expertise back into his organisation.

HOW DO YOU DEVELOP YOUR TEAM?

Will you choose to become the kind of leader who develops their people and whom no-one wants to leave? If so, carving out time with each of your people one on one to hold development conversations where you establish development goals, foster new habits, celebrate their successes and provide feedback for improvement is critical. Let's look at how we do this.

Development conversations

Like nearly everything you do as a leader, you'll discover that development also occurs in conversations with your team members. When I work with organisations, whether they're global or local, family businesses or public sector, I ask them, 'how do you develop your people?' I often hear things like:

- Well, we catch up twice a year ... OR
- Oh, I think we have an annual review ... OR
- Someone from HR sends me a form to fill in ...

When I hear those phrases, I have to check myself to make sure that I'm not *actually* groaning out loud and slamming my palm against my forehead! Part of me tries to be grateful that at least they are doing *something*, but if I'm honest I just start feeling frustrated at their lack of commitment to developing their people, who after all are the most valuable part of their organisation. An organisation without its people is completely useless. And an organisation which doesn't develop its people is going to be seriously underperforming. Think of all that untapped potential.

I feel very strongly that having regular development-centred conversations with your team members is one of *the* most important things you can do. And I'm not talking about tacking an extra five minutes on to your regular meeting each week; I'm talking about meeting with your team member for the sole purpose of discussing their development.

Development conversations form a cycle, as opposed to a linear process. This cycle is continuous. It commences when the team member joins your team and concludes (for you) when the team member leaves your team. As the pair of you discover a development need, you and your team member reflect on what action can be taken to fulfil that need and then put that action in place. Then as the team member develops to the next level, this cycle – which we'll dig into shortly – begins again with the next development need, and so on.

Depending on each team member's development stage these conversations may happen very frequently or may be spaced quite far apart. What I can share with you is that a one-off 'annual event' is not going to be enough. The problem with mandating how often development conversations occur (annually, quarterly, six-monthly) is that it doesn't consider individual development needs. Once a quarter may be too frequent for some and way too infrequent for others. Think of the difference between a brand-new team member and a team member who is well established in your team and often acts as your replacement when you're on leave – totally different development needs. As the leader, you need to work with each of your team members to determine when the next conversation should occur. Rather than locking yourself into a forced pattern, simply think about when the next conversation should occur. It may be:

- after a particular action has been completed
- after your team member has had a chance to practise a new habit
- before your team member attempts something new or challenging
- when your team member gets stuck with a development activity they're currently working on.

If you're always locking in the next development conversation when you're having the current one, you'll find that they are happening at just the right time, and of course you can be flexible and adjust them if things change.

Hopefully you're starting to build a picture of what the cycle of development conversations looks like now and how the frequency of the conversations will vary depending on each team member's needs. Let's get down to brass tacks; when you're actually inside one of those development conversations, what would that look like?

Inside a development conversation

A development conversation consists of three specific components: Discovery, Reflection and Action. (*Sound familiar?*) As you know, we use the three-letter acronym DRA.

DRA

Let me tell you the story of how DRA was developed. My delightful colleague Jillian (JD to her friends), when not designing fabulous programs for our clients, spends some of her time each year with her husband, Ross, on international house sits. They love looking after people's pets and properties, especially when they are in locations that they haven't explored before. One year JD and Ross went to Norway at the end of Norway's freezing winter to housesit a property perched by the side of a frozen lake. In preparation for the trip JD had started to learn Norwegian – which is no mean feat, I can tell you! While JD housesits, she continues to work, and we joke that our business has a 24/7 operation at those times, due to the different time zones we are working in. Anyway (I digress!), we were working on the design of a reflective process for one of our favourite clients and JD came up with the acronym DRA. In Norwegian, JD informed me, dra (pronounced 'drah') can mean 'to go' in the sense of 'to go on a journey' from once place to another. We thought this was pretty neat and brought the two together – if you want 'to go' somewhere (develop) you need to DRA.

Let's break down DRA and see what each part means.

D for Discovery

When you're in Discovery mode you are uncovering things. Like an explorer you are metaphorically looking closely at things (in this case your team members), picking up rocks and having a good look at what's underneath. You and your team member are attempting to discover things about the team member together. You might be looking for what the team member's strengths are, or what their challenges are. You might be discovering what their aspirations are – what do they want to be when they grow up? You might be discovering what went wrong in a recent 'fall' your team member experienced. You might be discovering what went right in a recent win. Wherever you place your attention, the two of you can dig deep with your discussion and unearth some treasures! Open questions will be your best friend when you're in Discovery mode. Once you have made your discovery, you have identified 'what' you're working on.

Let's have a look at two examples, so you can see how this works:

- Iluka is keen to make the move from his current expert role in the call centre to team manager, where he would lead the team directly. During a development conversation with his leader, Iluka discovers that he finds the thought of delivering feedback for improvement to potential team members terrifying! Iluka feels that this could be his biggest barrier to progression into the team manager role.

- Lucy wants to build her responsibilities from labouring in a construction team to being able to run a construction worksite herself. During a development conversation with her leader, Lucy discovers that she's most concerned about the Work Health & Safety aspects of the job as she feels a bit overwhelmed by the administration involved given her limited literacy skills. Lucy just can't see how she can overcome this in the short term, even though she's currently enrolled in a literacy program at the local TAFE.

R for Reflection

Once you've made a discovery and found 'what' you are working on, the next step is to move into reflection mode. Reflection is what you do to identify the 'so what'. Reflection is all about stepping back. Remember our dancefloor/balcony analogy? Reflection will have you sitting right up on the balcony, having a good look around. Reflection is introspective; meaning the team member looks inside – at their thoughts, feelings and previous experiences – for answers. You can use your newfound coaching skills to guide your team member through this introspection. Your team member's previous experience offers rich learning, where you can tap into it. And when you coach your team member you support them to become a more proficient reflector. You can also provide some insights from your perspective – what do you think, feel and/or observe about the situation? Let's see how this next part might look:

- As Iluka and his leader reflect on his fear of providing feedback for improvement, they uncover that in Iluka's previous team, the leader was very blunt and frequently upset team members when he provided feedback and didn't follow up to see that the team members were okay. Iluka remembers seeing what damage this caused the team, and is worried that if he doesn't get it right he might have the same effect on his team. Iluka also realises that there are two issues that he's currently avoiding talking to one of his colleague's about for the same reason.
- As Lucy and her leader reflect on Lucy's concern about the Work Health & Safety aspects of the job set up, they uncover that Lucy's worried she's going to miss something and place her workmates in danger. Lucy's leader also asks whether Lucy's lack of formal

qualifications is impacting her self-confidence, even though she has complete faith in her capabilities. Lucy says it is.

Once you have elicited some useful reflections, you are ready for the next step; action!

A for Action

If Discovery takes you to the 'what', and Reflection takes you to the 'so what', then Action helps you identify 'now what'. It's important to remember that development conversations are just fluff and bubble *unless* they move your team member to action. What needs to happen now? What are you going to do differently? What behaviour do you need to change? What learning do you need to undertake? When you're working on identifying the action, again you will be using your coaching skills to help your team member identify the action for themselves. If they've exhausted everything they have and can't come up with anything by themselves (which is *very* unlikely) then you can feel free to suggest something. Let's see how this final part of DRA looks in practice:

- Following a good brainstorming session on options, Iluka and his leader agree that the best course of action will be:
  a. For the leader to teach Iluka a feedback structure that he can use to provide the feedback to his colleague today.
  b. Then Iluka will prepare for the conversation and run through his ideas for the conversation as a role play with his leader before running the actual conversation with his colleague by the end of the week.
  c. Then Iluka will have the conversation with his colleague followed by a debrief with his leader on how it went early next week.
- Following an interesting discussion, Lucy and her leader agree that the best course of action will be:
  a. For Lucy to journal at the end of each day three things she did well as a way of increasing her self-confidence and practising her writing skills and share these with her leader at the end of each week.
  b. For Lucy and the leader to jointly create a WH&S job site set up checklist that Lucy can start using for guidance this week.

c. For Lucy to become responsible for using the WH&S checklist on existing jobs, under the supervision of her leader, for the next two months.

d. For Lucy to run a new small project worksite herself, that starts in two months' time, as a trial project.

You can see how these development conversations can be very powerful. They dig in deep to what's actually going on and orient your team member to taking action. They help you set up your team members for success and keep them learning and growing. Then, once you've completed your first DRA cycle, you just keep on repeating. The second cycle will begin with what your team member discovered from their initial set of actions and so their development continues. You're now on your way to developing your team members – excellent!

FEEDBACK

A large part of development conversations is about identifying the team member's development goal. Another large proportion is spent providing feedback. This can be nerve wracking for you as a new leader. Let's see if we can set you up for success.

Let's start with a story.

I was standing by the side of the soccer pitch with a friend, let's call him Patrick*, as we watched our 13-year-old sons battle out a six-a-side match one afternoon. Prior to starting my own business in 2013 we'd worked in the same organisation, but in different teams.

'How's it going at work?' I asked.

'Oh, I had my performance review today …' he said, gesticulating quotation marks in the air around the words 'performance review'. He piqued my interest.

'How did it go?' I said, genuinely curious.

'Well, I said to my manager – it's time for my performance review today.'

He said, 'Oh yeah?' And then added 'I think you're going good.'

'Anything else?' Patrick had asked.

'No that's it. All good. I think we're done.'

'And that's all he said,' he concluded, looking both disappointed and frustrated.

As you might appreciate, my poor friend was quite deflated by his feedback, or lack thereof. I share this story as sadly it is a very common experience inside organisations. It is a perfect entry for the Book of What Not to Do.

So, what are you going to do instead? You are a leader, and as such you are going to provide rich feedback to your team members. You could say that your feedback will be five-star feedback as we're going to use the acronym STAR to construct excellent feedback for your people.

There are two types of feedback you can provide to your team members; positive feedback, about something your team member has done well; and feedback for improvement, where there is an opportunity to do something better the next time.

Positive feedback

When one of your team does something well it's important to recognise what they've done and how they've done it. Recognition is so powerful as it demonstrates to your team members that you are paying attention to what they are doing, you're noticing their good work and that you care enough to take the time to give them feedback. As a quick rule of thumb, when you see something, say something. In addition, you want your team to be really clear on the positive behaviours that you would like them to do *more of.* When they don't know what they've done well, they won't know what to repeat to continue to be successful into the future.

A friend of mine worked for many years for one of Australia's premier resorts. They recalled a story of a manager there who was nick-named 'Good Job'! This manager spent his day walking around the resort saying 'Good job!', 'Good job!' to everyone. Before long his feedback, if you could call it that, meant nothing to the recipients. His intention was good – he wanted to recognise people for the work they were doing – but his delivery was poor and his feedback became meaningless. Have you ever encountered a 'Good job!' manager? I know earlier in my career I've fallen into this trap at times. The good news is that it is easy to deliver positive feedback to recognise your team.

To ensure that you become a five-STAR leader, as opposed to a 'Good Job!' manager, you're going to have to make your feedback very specific. To do that we'll use the STAR acronym to guide us. (*Some of you may be familiar with STAR from recruitment processes, where you may have used STAR to develop behavioural interview responses. If so, you're going to find this even easier!*)

STAR

STAR stands for:

ST	Situation or Task	The context in which the positive action or behaviour took place.
A	Action	The action/behaviour of your team member.
R	Result	The result this action/behaviour achieved.

Here are some examples with the STAR components identified:

- For a call centre team member: Emily, I was listening to one of your calls yesterday, the one where you were dealing with that angry customer (ST). I was really impressed by the way you asked questions to really understand their issue even though they were irate. I noticed that as you took time to listen to them and really understand the problem (A) they became a lot calmer, and then you moved smoothly to resolve the issue for them (R).
- For a construction team member: Rohit, thanks for sorting out the supplies issue yesterday (ST). When we discovered that we didn't have enough scaffolding to finish the job I appreciated that you took the time to calculate what exactly we needed to finish and then contact the supplier to quickly get additional scaffolding delivered to the site (A). That saved us having to return to that worksite again tomorrow when we have a very tight schedule (R).
- For a cafe team member: Alex, remember that tricky customer yesterday who kept changing his mind with his order (ST)? I appreciated how you stayed calm even though you had to change the order three times,

and that you took the time to explain the dishes to him so that he knew exactly what he was ordering (A). He had a great experience and ended up writing us an awesome review on Instagram (R).

- For a finance team member: Wow! That auditor really kept us on our toes, didn't they, Poorwa?! Congratulations on all the work you did to prepare for the audit (ST); the way you presented the information and had everything available at your fingertips for the auditor really made things run smoothly (A). The auditor was impressed with your professionalism and we've passed the audit with flying colours (R). I'm really grateful for your assistance.

Now have a play with STAR. What's a recent example of something one of your team members has done well? What was the situation or task? What action did they take that was useful? And what was the result they achieved? Put that altogether and you can deliver some five-STAR feedback to your team members. To begin with you might want to take some time to prepare your feedback, and as you practise it will become easier and easier.

You can even notice feedback that other people are giving. Maybe your leader gives you feedback. Is it five-STAR? If not, what component is missing? Perhaps you could share your learnings about five-STAR feedback with them so they can improve too?

In addition to providing STAR feedback, you need to think about how and when to deliver this feedback. Not everyone likes to be in the spotlight when they receive feedback. What do you notice about the team member you are about to give feedback to? Are they the kind of person who would appreciate a quiet word, one on one after work about what they did well? Or would they love you to shout it from the rooftops in the middle of a team meeting?

Leadership tip: share the love

When someone comes to you and shares some positive feedback about one of your team, as well as thanking them for giving the feedback you can ask them to provide the feedback to your team member directly. And you can also mention to your team member what the person said. That way they receive positive feedback twice!

And flipping this around, if you notice a team member in another team doing something well, give them the feedback directly and tell their leader as well!

Feedback for improvement

What about when things are not going so well and you need to give your team member some feedback to help them improve? Now, I know what you're thinking; oh, this is tough, I find it really difficult mustering the courage to do this. You may even start backing quietly into the nearest corner, yes? I know this is trickier, but you *can* totally do this! And I'm here to support you.

We're going to use STAR again with two slight modifications; an additional A and another AR at the end, to make it STAAR/AR! If you want to make this revised acronym for feedback for improvement stick in your head, then you can read it with your best pirate accent and roll the Rs to great effect: 'STAARrrrrr/ARrrrrr me hearties!' Try to give the feedback without the rum if you can! Random, interesting fact: did you know that when pirates used the term 'me hearties' it was to give due respect to a person for bravery or other admirable qualities? It's just like an ancient form of 'props'!

I think bravery is exactly what's called for when you're giving feedback for improvement; you're being brave to have what can sometimes be a tricky conversation with someone for their benefit. Being brave is a great start, and now let's talk a bit more about your mindset for providing feedback for improvement. I'd like to change the way you think about providing feedback for improvement and make you super keen to grasp this model and deliver it effectively, every time, to your team members.

Imagine this:

You are working in a new role, doing the best you can with your existing knowledge and skills and working hard. Unbeknown to you, you are making a really common 'rookie mistake' and, again unbeknown to you, you are irritating the rest of your team. Interestingly,

your leader sees you making these repeated errors but doesn't want
to bring it to your attention because they are worried that they will:

a. dampen your enthusiasm in the new role
b. damage their relationship with you
c. upset you
d. cause grief between you and your fellow team members.

As you continue (unaware that you are repeatedly making the same
mistake) you start to feel that there is 'an issue' between you and the
rest of the team, but you can't quite put your finger on it. As time goes
on an atmosphere starts to develop and coming to work in this team
seems to be losing its shine ...

Let's stop right there. Can you see where this is heading? Short answer:
nowhere good. You're on the downward spiral to disengagement. How
would you feel if you really were in that situation? Perplexed, confused,
unsupported, 'at sea' and the list goes on. The leader in this scenario is
neglecting their duty to develop their team member. Have I got your attention now? I hope so.

So, listen up! This is really important. Whenever *you* fail to provide
feedback for improvement, you are *preventing* your team member's development and growth. And yes, I really did say 'preventing'. What I would
like you to remember every single time you provide feedback for improvement to your team member is that you are providing this feedback to help
them learn and grow. You're not providing it to make them feel bad, you're
not providing it to discipline them, you're not providing it to put them in
their place, you're providing feedback for improvement for learning and
growth.

If your leader sat down with you and said, 'May I provide you with some
feedback to support you to learn and grow and become even better than
you are now?', what would you say?

Option A: 'No thank you, I'm fine'; or ...

Option B: 'Sure thing, bring it on!'

I think, if you're the kind of person who chose to read this book, it would
be option B. And this is what you need to do for your people – provide as
many opportunities as you can for them to learn and grow.

How are you feeling about giving feedback for improvement now? Better? Good work, let's do this thing!

Leadership tip: framing your feedback

I'd strongly recommend that you use the framing that feedback for improvement is exactly that; an opportunity for learning and growth, at the beginning of any of your feedback for improvement conversations. This is a reminder for you *and* your team members that your only intent here is to develop the person you are providing feedback too.

Before we get into the STAAR/AR method, let me share a story with you about what can happen when you decide to step into the challenge of providing feedback for improvement.

I was working with one of my clients delivering a leadership program to their emerging and existing leaders. Prior to this program I'd been working with the executive team on their development journey and I'd invited members of the executive team to join us and share their learnings about providing feedback for improvement to their own teams.

One of the executive team, Aykut*, led one of the larger divisions and explained that he'd been having a difficult time with Jo*, one of his direct reports. Jo's performance had been a bit sporadic over the last six months or so, and while Aykut had previously tried to work with Jo to remove blockers to Jo's performance and figure out a positive way forward, things had again been slipping. This time around, following our work together, Aykut decided to take a different approach.

Aykut shared with the group that he had called Jo in for a discussion, and used the framing technique to ensure that Jo knew the meeting was to help Jo succeed in the role and identify any opportunities for learning and growth. And this time Aykut suggested that perhaps to begin with Jo might like to share what Aykut could do differently to support Jo more.

'Well, Jo UNLOADED!' Aykut said, with a deer-in-the-headlights look on his face. 'It was like I was in the crosshairs and Jo just kept on firing!' he added. Aykut paused, and then continued, 'BUT it was really good, he just shared with me how he felt about how we were working – or should I say NOT working – together and what he thought I might do differently so that I could support him more. It was a really honest conversation.'

After that Aykut shared with Jo his observations about Jo's performance and together they developed a game plan to turn things around. 'That conversation was really honest, it was really tough, but really honest, and I felt afterwards we had a much better connection and guess what? Jo's performance has really lifted ... it's been amazing.'

What a turnaround!

I would love you to hold this story (and it's a real one, like all the other stories in this book – names changed here for obvious reasons) in your mind, particularly on those days when you're wavering about providing feedback for improvement. Every time you provide feedback for improvement you are offering your team member the opportunity to learn and grow; to deepen their knowledge, to develop their skills, to refine their behaviours, to tap into new and exciting opportunities. If you don't, you run the risk of anchoring them firmly in their current position, stuck fast with only their existing skills and knowledge.

Let's now have a look at the STAAR/AR model. You can use STAAR/AR in two different ways:

1. To support a team member to bounce back from a fall (alternate action and result).
2. To stretch them even further when they are going well (additional action and result).

BOTH of these options are feedback for improvement.

As you already know, the STAR acronym stands for Situation or Task, Action and Result. And this time we are adding on three more letters; an extra A and an extra AR at the end.

STAAR/AR

ST	Situation or Task	The context in which the action or behaviour took place.
A	ASK	Ask your team member for their perspective on the situation.
A	Action	The action/behaviour of your team member.
R	Result	The result this action/behaviour achieved.
A	ALTERNATE ACTION	What the team member can do differently.
R	ALTERNATE RESULT	What result the team member will achieve instead.
OR		
A	ADDITIONAL ACTION	What additional action the team member can take.
R	ADDITIONAL RESULT	What additional result the team member will achieve.

Rebounding after a fall

Let's start with supporting your team member to bounce back after a fall. As with positive feedback we're going to start with the Situation/Task as context for our feedback. Let's work through an example together. Let's use our cafe scenario, where the leader is having a conversation with one of the waitstaff, Meiying, to work this through.

We'll begin with the Situation/Task to set the scene:

Leader: Hey Meiying, could we please have a talk about the mixed-up order issue you had with the couple on table 12?

M: Sure, I remember that one.

And then we'll move onto the Ask:

Leader: What happened there?

M: Well, they couldn't make up their mind about what they were ordering, so I had to change their order a few times, but by the end I felt I was clear on what they had ordered and I put the order through to the kitchen. Then when I came back to their table, they said that wasn't what they wanted. And I had to do another order.

Now we're moving onto Action:

Leader: Okay. Let's just make sure I've got this straight. So, you listened to their order, and they kept changing their minds and you were adjusting the order on the tablet and then when you thought you were clear you submitted the order, right?

M: Yep. That's it.

Now we're moving onto Result:

Leader: And what was the result of that?

M: Well, they didn't want the meals I thought they'd ordered, as they said they had ordered something else so I had to order another two meals from the kitchen and the two original meals were wasted. And the kitchen was pretty busy, so the re-order made it even busier and the customers had to wait longer for their meals. And then the customers were pretty grumpy.

Next comes the Alternate Action:

Leader: What do you think you could do differently next time to get a better result?

M: Look, I don't really know, they were just annoying customers, you know ...

Leader: I appreciate it was a challenging situation, and I'd like to suggest that when you're taking orders, especially with people who keep changing their minds, that at the end of their order you read the order back to them so that you are clear and they are clear on what was ordered. How does that sound?

M: Yeah, that sounds pretty straightforward.

And then we finish with the Alternate Result:

Leader: When we read back the orders to the customers, we'll know that they are crystal clear on what they've ordered, it will reduce pressure on the kitchen, the customers will be happier as we'll get things right first time around, which will also make it a more enjoyable experience for you and we'll reduce costs as we don't waste any meals. What, if anything, do you need from me Meiying to support you?

M: Got it. Can you just show me how to review the whole order at once on the tablet again please so I can read it back to the customer?

Leader: Sure thing …

As you read through the scenario, what did you notice? Hopefully you noticed that we asked a few questions along the way:

- What happened?
- What was the result?
- What do you think you could do differently next time to get a better result?
- What, if anything, do you need from me to support you?

Asking clarifying questions as you work through feedback for improvement is how you bring your coaching approach to feedback. It ensures that you don't jump to conclusions, that you understand the situation from your team member's perspective and that you are working with your team member to help them learn and grow. In the example above, Meiying didn't really have any ideas on how to improve the next time, so the leader made a suggestion. When you are working with your team members you may find that they are full of improvement ideas, some that are even better than yours! Make sure you ask them first as they will be more committed to something they have suggested. Also make sure that you have some ideas of your own so that you can support them if they don't have any idea how to move forward.

Get into the habit of asking the question 'What support do you need from me?' at the end of a feedback conversation to make sure you're clear on what you can do differently to support your team member.

Stretch

What if your team member is going really well AND you can see an opportunity for them to stretch even more? This can be really powerful feedback – if you're already giving your team members this type of feedback, give yourself 10/10 for being in the Development Zone! Go you! If you haven't done this before, let's walk through an example. What you'll notice this time is that as it's a stretch opportunity we're going to go for an Additional Action and an Additional Result instead of Alternate Action and Alternate Result, as we did in the previous example. This time we'll jump into the world of the call centre where a leader is having a conversation with one of their inbound sales consultants, Riaan:

We'll begin with the Situation/Task to set the scene:

Leader: Hey Riaan, I've just been looking at your stats for this week and listening to some of your calls and I can see that you are smashing it out of the park! Great work.

R: Thanks so much. Yes, I'm feeling pretty good about how things are going right now.

And then we'll move onto the Ask:

Leader: What do you think is helping you achieve these great results?

R: Well, I think now I've got more experience with customers, I've been changing my style to adapt more to the styles of the customers and that seems to be helping me connect better with them.

Now we're moving onto Action:

Leader: That's great Riaan, well done. I also notice that you've got an excellent understanding of the products that we offer.

R: Oh thanks. Yes, I've been brushing up on my product knowledge a bit lately!

Now we're moving onto Result:

Leader: And what do you think has been the benefit of this?

R: I reckon knowing the products well means that I know the potential benefits to the customer, and when I make recommendations that I feel are right for them they seem to really appreciate my expertise in guiding them to a good solution that fits their needs.

Leader: That's awesome, and I can see that you've had the highest sales for the last four weeks as well! So, it's a win/win; a win for the customer and a win for the business.

Next comes the Additional Action:

Leader: Given that you're going so well, what else might you like to do to stretch yourself just a little bit more?

R: Well, I heard that our team expert is going on leave in a few weeks and I was wondering if I might be able to step into her position for two weeks and see if I could learn some of the expert skills. What do you think?

Leader: Awesome idea!

R: Great!

And then we finish with the Additional Result:

Leader: What do you think might be the benefits of relieving in the expert role, for you and the team?

R: Well, if I start with the team, I think I'd be able to share some of my knowledge and skills to help them perform as well as I am at the moment. And for me, I'd like to apply for an expert position in six months or so and this would give me an opportunity to learn a lot and see if I like the position and to identify what else I might have to learn to get ready for the role.

Leader: Couldn't have said it better myself! What support do you need from me to get going?

R: Could we set up a meeting between you, me and our expert to talk about how this might work?

Leader: Absolutely. How does next Wednesday work in your diary ... ?

Again, you would have noticed that we asked lots of questions, enabling the team member to drive their own development with some gentle guidance from us along the way. Powerful stuff, hey?! Remember that when we talk about the Result, that can be the result for the team member, or the team, or the organisation, or the customer, or even the result for the leader – you can make as many connections as is useful to reinforce the benefits of the particular course of action. The more you make, the more powerful your message.

In the example above you would have noticed that the leader coached the additional action and result out of Riaan. Riaan came up with his own suggestion and realised the results this might bring. Sometimes you might have a team member who's not clear on what else they could do, or who makes a suggestion that is not possible to move forward with at that time. Either way, it's useful if you have spent some time thinking about potential actions and results prior to the conversation. This demonstrates that you've put some effort into thinking about your team member's development and shows you're invested in them.

There you have it. You now have the STAR and STAAR/AR models at your fingertips so that you can provide really helpful and constructive positive feedback and feedback for improvement to your team members and avoid becoming a 'Good Job!' manager!

HOW MUCH FEEDBACK SHOULD I PROVIDE?

One thing new leaders often ask is how much feedback is enough? The first thing I'd say is that I've never met anyone who told me that they receive too much feedback. Can you imagine the conversation … ?

HR Manager:	Thanks for attending this exit interview with me. I'm really interested to know what's contributed to you leaving?
Team Member:	Well, it's my manager you know …
HR Manager:	THINKS *As I suspected, it's always the damn manager!* SAYS: 'Oh, yes? Please go on …'

Team Member: Well, it's just that they're always providing feedback, they take the time to share with me what I'm doing well and what I can improve. They're really specific and usually they try and coach me through it myself, so I come up with my own ideas. And if I can't think of anything, they usually have some good ideas that I can take on. And frankly, I'm just over it. They're just *too* invested in me and believe that I can become excellent in my role and step up in the future for promotion as well and it's just really *too* much ...

... SAID NO-ONE EVER!

Seriously though now, how much is enough? The answer (annoyingly!) is 'it depends'. Consider this:

- If your team member is new and is learning their role, they may need significant amounts of positive feedback to reassure them that they are going well and doing the right things, and of course they will need feedback for improvement *when*, and I emphasise the *when*, they fall down.
- If your team member is established in their role, I'm sure they will still appreciate positive feedback – this is likely to be for more significant achievements, not just learning the basics of how to get the job done like the new team member. They are likely to be more interested in feedback for improvement; how do I get to the next stage? How do I take on more responsibility in my current role? As they become more experienced, they start to look for the stretch – the additional action and the additional result.

So, the best option is to ask each team member how you're going with providing feedback. Use the Goldilocks principle: Too little? Too much? Or, just right? Let them guide you.

How do I tailor my feedback so that it's 'just right' for each team member?

Feedback needs to be delivered in a way that is best suited to the individual. Different team members like to receive feedback differently, and your duty as a leader is to figure this out quickly so that you can deliver feedback in the way most suited to each person. And if you have five team members you may need to deliver feedback in five different ways. Back to flexing your style again, right?

The most useful thing you can do here is take time to sit down with each of your team members individually and ask them the following questions and note their responses:

- *Where* do you prefer to receive your feedback – in public or privately?
- In *what medium* do you prefer to receive your feedback – face to face or in writing?
- *How direct* would you prefer your feedback to be – blunt or diplomatic?
- *How soon* would you prefer to receive your feedback – immediately or give me time to sleep on it?
- How would you prefer me to *act afterwards*? Check in or move on?

Let's explore each of these questions in turn.

Where does your team member prefer to receive your feedback?

Your delivery choices here are public or private. There are many versions of 'public'; from team meetings to awards nights, from meeting notes to CEO weekly videos. When I talk about private, what I mean is a one-to-one conversation with the team member directly, usually out of earshot of other people.

For those who prefer to receive their positive feedback in public, they may appreciate it if you acknowledge their good work in a team meeting or in one of your internal publications, or via the intranet and the like.

You may even find that some people are happy to receive their feedback for improvement in a public or team setting. Where there is high trust among the team, team members can become more and more comfortable about receiving feedback for improvement in front of the team. This can take some time to build, so when you're just beginning to lead, I'd recommend delivering feedback for improvement in private until you discover otherwise from the person directly, or feel that you are ready to take feedback delivery in your team to the next level.

Others can feel embarrassed about receiving positive feedback in public. They may hate the feeling of being 'in the spotlight', and it is important that you respect their wishes and perhaps just have a quiet word with them about what specifically they did well, using the STAR framework. If you have a team member who prefers to receive feedback in private you may have to educate others in the organisation about this. Perhaps this team member is up for an organisational award and they are expected to attend an awards night, which feels to them like a form of torture! What creative ideas can you come up with to support your team member in a situation like this? If you recognise someone who prefers feedback delivered privately in a public way, you're possibly diluting, or negating, the benefit for the person.

Remember what I said earlier: Treat others the way THEY would like to be treated.

In *what medium* does your team member prefer to receive your feedback?

Basically, there are two options here: face to face or in writing.

Face-to-face feedback is very powerful. And I'd recommend that as far as you possibly can – and taking your team member's preferences into account – you attempt to provide most, if not all, of your feedback face to face. When I say face to face, I include virtual face-to-face methods, like Zoom, Google Meet, Microsoft Teams, Skype or even FaceTime. Being able to have a conversation about the feedback is very powerful – you can't coach your team member through feedback for improvement if you've written it down! Being able to read your team member's body language, hear their tone of voice and observe the ups and downs of the conversation is incredibly useful to you as a leader.

At times you may like to provide written feedback, which may include a handwritten note, an email, an instant message or text. You can get more creative – a post-it note on their desk, a flip chart on the wall, a Jamboard or electronic whiteboard in your training room and more! The benefit of placing positive feedback in writing is that the person can review the feedback again and again and hopefully really take in the positive words you have written.

Think very carefully about this if you're considering placing feedback for improvement in writing – dwelling on what can sometimes be *perceived* by the team member as a negative when things have not gone quite to plan is not really a good thing. Feedback for improvement is best done face to face. That said, if your team member really wishes feedback for improvement written down so they can think deeply about it and implement changes for the future, you could do this after you've had the initial discussion with them.

How *direct* would your team member prefer your feedback to be?

Some team members just like to hear things as they are – to the point, straightforward, no fluff, however you wish to describe it. With them you can just cut to the chase. Often if you have known your team member for a while and have an established relationship, or even a new relationship with a strong connection, you can call things out easily and directly. Again, just stick to the STAR and STAAR/AR frameworks to deliver your message and all will go well.

If your team member prefers more diplomatic feedback, you still use the STAR or STAAR/AR frameworks, and I'd suggest strongly that you stick to your coaching approach with lots of questions to land this feedback well.

When you use the STAR and STAAR/AR frameworks your feedback will be both to the point *and* diplomatic at the same time. When you maintain the mindset that your role as a leader is to support your team members to learn and grow, I am confident your feedback will be received positively.

How *soon* would your team member prefer to receive your feedback?

Again, two options here. Does your team member prefer feedback immediately or would they like a little time to process things before having the conversation?

Generally, it is best to provide feedback in a timely fashion. If you leave it for three weeks after the event has occurred to provide feedback your team member may:

- have difficulty recalling the situation
- be disappointed that you didn't provide positive feedback at the time – they may think, why didn't they notice that great result I achieved?
- be frustrated that you didn't provide feedback for improvement at the time – they may think, why didn't they tell me then, so I could have done something about it?
- feel all of the above!

If you have a team member who prefers feedback straight away you can just get straight to it.

If you have a team member who prefers a bit of time to process the situation, you may like to give them a heads up that you wish to have a conversation about a particular situation with them the following day, so they can prepare themselves overnight and get their thoughts together. You can reinforce that the discussion is, as always, around supporting them to learn and grow and that you'll be interested to hear their insights the following day.

In my mind, I think that even team members who like a little time to process can handle receiving positive feedback very quickly, it's more the feedback for improvement where you need to allow a little processing time. That said, some people like to circle back and have another conversation about the positive feedback and that brings us to our next question.

How would your team member prefer you to act afterwards?

Picture this: you've provided feedback to your team member; you've used the frameworks and you feel like you have landed the feedback and had a really good discussion. They seem to have understood everything. As you quietly pat yourself on the back, you think to yourself, 'Feedback delivered, learnings identified, job done!' Right?

Well, maybe. Or ... maybe not.

This was the thought a client of mine – an extroverted, vivacious, big picture (i style) leader – was having not so long ago after she'd had what she thought had been a great feedback conversation with one of her more introverted, mild mannered, detail orientated (C style) team members. As the leader was metaphorically dusting her hands and ready to move onto the next issue for the day, unbeknown to the leader her team member was quietly considering that this was just the first of several conversations about the topic.

'Oh gosh, I thought we were just getting started,' she shared in a later conversation.

This discussion came out during a breakout discussion at a Building Relationships workshop I was running with the organisation's executive team and their direct reports, which looked at different behavioural styles. In this particular session, we were discussing how people with opposite style preferences communicate differently.

It was fabulous to watch the lightbulb moment when the leader had a deep insight about the fact that how she preferred to operate – providing feedback and then closing out that conversation and moving on – was *not* the way her team member preferred to operate, which was to revisit the initial conversation again later to ensure that any further thoughts could be shared and any wrinkles ironed out.

So, you can see how important it is to find out whether your team member prefers to just have the conversation and then move on, or whether they prefer you to check back in and find out whether they have further insights, questions or observations that they'd like to share. It will be fascinating for you to find out what your different team members' preferences are in relation to this question.

I appreciate that this may feel daunting at first, as there is quite a bit of discovery you have to do with each of your team members to find out their feedback preferences. Be assured that if you take the time to find this out, you will really be setting yourself and your team up for success and you will be in the best possible position to provide feedback that keeps each team member learning and growing. It doesn't get better than that, does it?!

The more you practise the easier it will become – remember the four stages of learning from chapter 1? You may be starting at conscious incompetence (*See! By reading this book you've already moved up one level – BONUS!*), but before you know it you will have moved up to conscious competence, and then you'll transition to providing five-STAR feedback automatically!

Now you need to practise.

WHAT IFS: COMMON CHALLENGES AND HOW TO OVERCOME THEM

I hope after reading through this fourth duty of leadership you are feeling a lot clearer about developing your team members. What it means, the difference between training and development, and how to go about having powerful development conversations with your people. Maybe you've still got a few questions? Here are my answers to a few common 'what ifs' that may help.

What if your organisation's development process sucks?

Having read this chapter, you may have a few alarm bells going off. You may be thinking, 'Uh ohhh! We're one of those organisations that has annual or six-monthly reviews! Now what am I going to do?' ... accompanied by the dull thud of your head hitting your desk.

Not to worry!

While you may be required to document your six monthly or annual conversations with your team members there is nothing to stop you having MORE conversations! Just follow the steps outlined in this chapter, and when you get to your formal review, capture your progress to date in your review process. I suspect you'll find that your team is developing in leaps and bounds, and HR and your manager will be wondering how your team is developing so well and so quickly compared to other teams when you're only meeting twice a year! (*It can be our little secret!*)

You can explain to your team members that you believe development conversations are essential to their success and therefore you want to have them more often, and you can share how you're going to link in what you're doing to the existing process in your organisation. I've never heard of a leader being reprimanded for developing their team too much. If that has ever happened to you, it's time to find a new employer!

What if your organisation has no formal development process?

Perhaps you're leading in a small business or a start-up where your systems are not yet developed. That's okay. Lots of people have that experience, and as a small business owner and a leader myself I know what it's like to grow and then find that you need a whole new set of systems to support your growing organisation. You don't need to make things complicated. We have developed some simple resources that you can access via our bonus resources page at the back of the book to get you started.

After all, it's just a conversation. Prepare some notes to support you through the DRA cycle, jot down some really good questions you want to ask, and you'll be off and running before you know it.

What if you have no team development budget?

Money can be tight in organisations. Sadly, in these situations, one of the budget items most commonly 'slashed' is the development budget. Maybe you call it the training budget in your business. Don't let that be a barrier – make it a challenge to think creatively about what development opportunities you can provide. Budget only becomes a problem if you think that development = training courses. But there are so many things you can do that don't involve outlaying money to provide development opportunities to your team.

Here's a great example from one of our national telecommunications providers. In this organisation they have a development opportunity called a 'Ride Along'. This is where a team member spends the day *riding along* with another team member in a different team. Think of it as 'a day in the life of' experience. They have an opportunity to see what the other team member does in their role, what that work involves, they may even get to participate in something depending on the work involved. They get to meet new people and understand a different element of the business, which broadens their understanding of what that role contributes to the business and how their own role interacts with the role they're learning about on the day. It's such an excellent development opportunity. And no financial outlay. Yes, you will be paying both people's salaries on the day, but you were paying for that anyway.

Here are some other examples of 'no budget' development:

- participation in a new project or activity
- mentoring by another team member in your organisation
- job swaps
- reading a book
- relieving in a peer's position when they're on leave
- doing research on something they don't know about
- creating a presentation on a topic and sharing it with peers

- teaching someone else how to do something
- watching TED Talks on a topic of interest.

I'm sure now I've got you started you can think of lots more too! AND ask your team members! What can they think of? I'm sure you'll come up with lots of great options.

What if your team member doesn't know what they want to be when they grow up?

My first response to this question is: does anyone? Okay, so that's a bit cheeky! Seriously now though, from my experience I would say that those people who know exactly what they want to be when they grow up are the exception rather than the rule. Personally, I love what I do, yet at 48 as I said earlier I am still asking myself that question! Some would say I have an addiction to development!

If you have someone who's not clear on what they want to do next, that can sometimes end up in a never-ending loop of a conversation that doesn't really go anywhere and we want to avoid that. Switch focus and ask them, 'What do you enjoy doing?' and 'What would you enjoy doing more?'. 'What have you enjoyed doing in the past?' can also be a useful question, especially if your team member seems to have lost their spark in their current role.

Sometimes it's useful to run some experiments. With an experiment it feels like a lower risk, for the person and for you. 'Let's just try this and see what happens – maybe you'll like it, maybe you won't – let's just see.' This can encourage your team member to dip their toe into a new pool and give something fresh a try.

What if I find myself having the same feedback conversation with a team member over, and over, and over ... ?

Sometimes when we have a conversation with a team member about an area for improvement, it doesn't quite land the first time. Maybe they made a bit of an improvement but didn't quite go the whole way, or maybe your message wasn't clear enough and they didn't quite understand what you were asking. Either way, you might need to have a second conversation to tidy up the rough edges. That's fair enough.

But what if you've had *exactly* the same conversation with them over and over and over again, and you're *certain* they're understanding you, but their behaviour isn't changing? This is what I call a 'Groundhog Day' conversation. (If you haven't seen the 1993 movie starring Bill Murray called *Groundhog Day*, basically Bill plays a weatherman covering an annual Groundhog Day event who becomes trapped in a time loop, forcing him to relive the same day over and over and over … and over … again.) The moment you find yourself thinking, 'Haven't we had this conversation before … ?' I want you to stop. When you're having a Groundhog Day conversation you are in the *wrong* conversation. There are actually two things going on here. Let's make it easy with an example:

Imagine that you have a team member who is repeatedly late for work. The first time it happened, you took them aside and used your STAAR/AR framework to have a feedback for improvement conversation with them, which you thought went well. But then a few days later it happened again. Weird. 'Well, I'd better have that conversation with them again,' you thought, 'to make sure that we're understanding each other and there's not a more serious issue going on here.' Good idea. All seemed well and your team member committed to be on time. But then, your team member is late for the third time, and by this stage you're starting to feel more than a little frustrated and perhaps a bit of 'tone' is creeping into the feedback for improvement conversation you're rehearsing in your mind. STOP right here. This 'Are you kidding me? Do I *really* have to have that conversation *again*?' feeling is the Groundhog Day alarm.

Two things are happening. The first issue (or conversation) is that your team member is frequently late. But now a second and more important issue has emerged – this team member is not responding to feedback for improvement. Now that really *is* a concern – it's a signal that you *may* have an uncoachable team member on your hands. So, instead of having *another* conversation about their tardiness, you need to get up on that balcony and have a good look down at what's really going on and have a STAAR/AR conversation about their lack of response to your previous feedback. The framing of the conversation may sound something like this:

> Thanks for meeting with me today. As you know, I feel it's my role to help you and everyone in my team to be their best. I've got a concern

which I'd like to bring to your attention, and it might be a bit of a tricky conversation for both of us, but the reason I'm sharing this with you is because if I don't, I'll be preventing you from improving and I won't be serving you well.

As you know we've already had two conversations about your punctuality and in our last discussion you committed to being on time. Today I noticed that you were 30 minutes late. So, this would be the third time we'd be discussing the same issue. This actually raises a different concern with me now, which is a slightly different conversation, and that is my concern that you are not responding and taking action on feedback for improvement.'

Then you'd move into the 'Ask' component of the framework, with your curious approach, focusing on the lack of action on feedback, as opposed to the 'being late' issue.

'What do you think might be getting in the way of you implementing your commitments?'

OR

'What's the real challenge here for you?'

OR

'What's actually going on here?'

Then you can progress through the rest of the STAAR/AR framework. Be careful not to get sucked back into the original issue – park it for now. While they are of course linked, the second issue – not responding to feedback – is far more serious than the first, and must be addressed, otherwise, like Bill Murray, you will find yourself and your team member trapped in the same conversation for eternity.

What do I do if my leader, or the organisation I work for, tells me that the best way to deliver feedback is to use the feedback sandwich approach?
The feedback sandwich – praising the team member, then giving them some feedback for improvement, and then giving them more praise at the end – also has another name. It's called the 'sh*t sandwich'. It has that name for a reason. I think it's because that's how you feel when you've swallowed it! It runs the risk of making you look insincere. There's also a high chance your team member didn't take away the feedback for improvement you intended. They only took away the positive feedback. It's murky, at best.

Don't meet with a team member with your list of five things they need to work on, and slap a bit of praise on either end. I'm pretty sure that would taste disgusting. You should be raising wins and opportunities with them as and when they arise – not saving them up. Use the STAR model for positive feedback and STAAR/AR model for feedback for improvement and you'll never have to serve up a sh*t sandwich again!

What if a team member doesn't want to develop?
This can be a tricky one as there can be a few different reasons for this. Let's look at three common ones:

1. I'm too old to learn.
2. I'm just about to retire.
3. I have nothing to learn.

Let's look at each of these.

What if a team member says they are just too old to learn?
Are team members ever really just too old to learn? In a word, no.

Do you remember at the beginning of the book we talked about mindsets – fixed and growth? If you choose a fixed mindset then you are choosing not to learn, even though you have the capacity to learn until the day you die. Neuroscience has proven the concept of neuroplasticity, which basically is the brain's ability to form new pathways and change its way of operating. Courtney Ackerman, who writes for Positive Pyschology. com and holds a Master's degree in positive organisational psychology and evaluation, explains:

The connection [between the growth mindset and neuroplasticity] is an important one.

The concepts mirror each other; a growth mindset is a mindset that one's innate skills, talents, and abilities can be developed and/or improved with determination, while neuroplasticity refers to the brain's ability to adapt and develop beyond the usual developmental period of childhood.

A person with a growth mindset believes that he or she can get smarter, better, or more skilled at something through sustained effort – which is exactly what neuroplasticity tells us. You might say that a growth mindset is simply accepting the idea of neuroplasticity on a broad level!

So, there we have it. Everyone, no matter what age, has the ability to learn (as long as they are in good mental health). Perhaps when you explain to them that they do have the ability to learn AND you believe that they can, they may be prepared to give it a try.

If not, and some choose not to develop, perhaps they have a fixed mindset. I'll be frank here: people with a fixed mindset are not really the people you want to have on your team. If you've had quite a few conversations with this person and they are adamant that they don't want to develop, then it may be time to part company.

What if my team member is just about to retire?
This is an awesome time for development, but in this situation, the team member who is retiring can develop others rather than undergoing development themselves. It's critical that you take the opportunity to encourage your retiring team member to pass on their knowledge, skills and wisdom to other team members or people inside the organisation before they go. This has two benefits. Firstly, you are acknowledging all the wisdom and experience that this team member has gathered over time and encouraging them to leave a lasting legacy by passing this on to another team member who can continue their work after they have retired. Secondly, you are ensuring that all that fantastic knowledge is retained inside

your organisation after your retiring team member has left. It's a win for everyone!

You may need to invest some time preparing and supporting your retiring team member to pass on their knowledge. Perhaps supporting them with delegation techniques and/or systems and processes to capture their knowledge.

What if my team member says they have nothing to learn?
ALARM *ALARM* *ALARM*
If you happen to have a large red button, with the words 'Eject' written on it, hidden under your desk, which opens a secret trapdoor under the seat that this team member is sitting on, HIT IT NOW!!

If you don't have one of those buttons (*dammit!*) read on for some more sensible advice.

Fortunately, the vast majority of people you will have in your team will be really receptive to your coaching approach; in fact, if you've been a bit of an advice-giving-manager in the past and can switch to becoming a leader with an awesome coaching approach, you're going to see them flourish under your new way of being.

But what if every time you or other team members work with one particular person they respond with a 'No, you're wrong. I'm going to do it my way' attitude? Well, you may have an uncoachable team member on your hands. When someone is uncoachable they have the attitude that they know better than everyone else (even if they actually don't) and that no-one else has any idea what they're talking about. You will notice a distinct lack of humility. (For more on this check out The Ideal Team Player, by Patrick Lencioni, in the Recommended Reading list)

For me this is a red flag of the most serious variety. No-one knows everything about everything. Even the smartest people in the world are lifelong learners continually looking for new things to learn and ways to improve how they're being and what they're doing.

If you discover someone is 'uncoachable', and I don't use this term lightly, then you need to bring this to their attention quickly and explain the impacts. If they show no desire to turn this around, it may be time to, as gracefully as you can, part ways.

DRA learning reflection

Discoveries:

- Training and development are both important, but they're not the same.
- Training relates to the specific knowledge, skills and competencies that your team member needs to perform effectively in their current role.
- Development is focused on the person's potential for growth and their future aspirations.
- Training and development engage your team members and help retain them in your organisation.
- Development can be so much more than a training program.
- Development can look very different for different team members; development is personal.
- Development conversations are a cycle of regular discussions about your team member's development needs and plan.
- Development conversations have three components – Discovery, Reflection and Action (DRA):
  - Discovery supports your team member to uncover which areas they would like to develop in.
  - Reflection supports your team member to think more deeply and differently about what they discovered and why that might be important.
  - Action supports your team member to implement the next steps to achieve their desired growth and learning.
- There are two types of feedback – positive feedback and feedback for improvement:
  - Use STAR to give positive feedback; something your team member has done well.

- Use STAAR/AR to give feedback for improvement; an opportunity for your team member to do something differently or even better the next time.
- Provide feedback in the way your team member would like to receive it.
- If you're having the same feedback for improvement conversation over and over with a team member, you're having the wrong conversation.

- Don't use the 'feedback sandwich' technique – it tastes nasty!

Reflection questions:

- On a scale of 1 to 10, with 1 low and 10 high, to what extent are you providing training and development opportunities for your team members?
- What might your team members say about the extent to which they are being developed and stretched?
- How regularly are you providing positive feedback to your team members?
- What are you seeing your team members do well, but not sharing with them yet?
- What tricky feedback for improvement conversation have you been avoiding and why?
- What is it that each of your team members needs to know now, so they can improve into the future?

Actions to choose from:

- When I'm having a development conversation with a team member, instead of waiting for the next 'annual review meeting', I will book in the next catch up before we finish that meeting.
- When I see my team member do something well, instead of just noticing it, I will give them some positive feedback using the STAR model the same day.
- When I see an area in which my team member could do better, instead of avoiding it, I will provide them with feedback for improvement using the STAAR/AR model by the end of that week.

'It seems that the necessary thing to do is not to fear mistakes, to plunge in, to do the best that one can, hoping to learn enough from blunders to correct them eventually.'

Abraham Harold Maslow

Chapter 13

YOUR FIFTH DUTY: RESOLVING PROBLEMS WITH YOUR TEAM

When I first started my business in 2013, there was just little old me. If a problem arose it was really simple: I solved it. Yes, I might have done some research or called out to someone I trusted outside my business to provide advice, but ultimately it was on me to work the issue through and come to a resolution.

Now, nearly eight years later I'm very fortunate to have six wonderful women sharing their many virtues and talents with me, each other and the clients we serve. Problem solving has become a little different.

In my business we create transparency around project management and facilitate file sharing using an application called SamePage. (*It ensures that we are 'on the same page' – clever name, I thought!*) Like most apps these days it has a 'chat' function and you can see the team discussing issues on particular projects in real time. Nothing new in that for most of you, I'm sure. One of my greatest delights I have to say though, has been watching my team solve their own problems together, *without* me. To me that feels like success. My team is empowered to make decisions to solve problems with each other and with our clients; they no longer need me to make the call. Don't get me wrong, there are still some issues or problems where it's on me to decide, but as time progresses my team are more and more empowered to work with each other to resolve problems.

UNDERSTANDING THIS DUTY

You may find this initially to be one of the most challenging duties of people leadership. This is because there is a significant shift required in how you go about resolving problems as a people leader and how you go about solving problems as the expert you were in your previous role. In your previous role you were an individual contributor – you only had yourself to worry about. Now you're a people leader, you've become responsible for a team of people.

In your previous role, if you encountered a problem your next action was pretty simple – you just thought about the answer, maybe you asked someone else for help, and then you took some action. Job done. Similarly, if someone came to you with a problem, it was your responsibility to resolve it and again you likely thought about the answer, did some research and then you provided the person with some advice about how to resolve *their* problem. Again, job done.

If you continue to use that strategy with your team you're going to run into a rather large problem. If you are the font of all knowledge, and you solve all their problems, your office will start to resemble the delicatessen counter at the supermarket with everyone 'taking a number' and waiting in line to seek *your* answers to *their* problems. In short, you will continue in your previous role of 'guru' and you will create a team of 'seekers' who are coming to you for alleged enlightenment!

How might you do this differently? Firstly, you need to think differently about your role in supporting your team to solve *their* problems. Notice I say, *their* problems, not *your* problems. Instead of being the expert or the guru handing out advice, you need to become the coach and start handing out lots of questions, through which your team will be able to solve their own problems. 'A-ha! I'll be providing questions, not answers!' you say? BINGO! You're placing that coaching hat squarely on your head and thinking of some great questions that will help your team members to work through their problems, consider them from different perspectives, generate some options and ultimately come up with a great set of actions to move them forward. When you move from advice giver to coach, you enable your team to become self-sufficient and help them realise that they do have the answers and that they are capable of resolving their own problems. Powerful stuff!

THE GROW MODEL

I'm going to share with you a really neat model you can use to work through problems with your team. It's a very well-known coaching model created by Sir John Whitmore and is ideal for beginners. It's called the GROW model, and the letters stand for Goal, Reality, Option, Wrap Up. One thing is for sure, when you start using the GROW model to support your team to resolve problems, you will be GROWing your people.

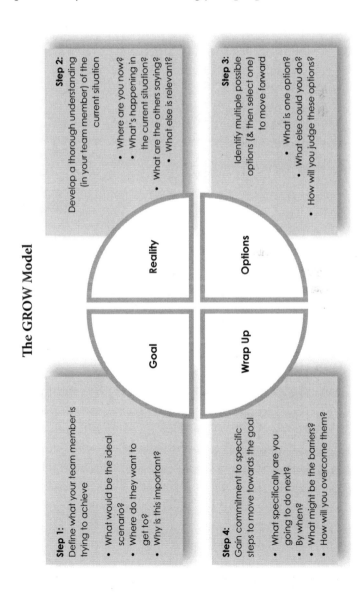

The GROW Model

Step 1:
Define what your team member is trying to achieve

- What would be the ideal scenario?
- Where do they want to get to?
- Why is this important?

Step 2:
Develop a thorough understanding (in your team member) of the current situation

- Where are you now?
- What's happening in the current situation?
- What are the others saying?
- What else is relevant?

Step 3:
Identify multiple possible options (& then select one) to move forward

- What is one option?
- What else could you do?
- How will you judge these options?

Step 4:
Gain commitment to specific steps to move towards the goal

- What specifically are you going to do next?
- By when?
- What might be the barriers?
- How will you overcome them?

Goal   Reality   Options   Wrap Up

Goal

So, let's start with G for Goal. When you're talking about the Goal, you're trying to help your team member discover the real problem to be solved, or the outcome that the person is working towards. If we use a holiday analogy, the Goal is Point B, it's your team member's destination. It's where they're trying to get to.

In my experience as an executive coach, what I often find is that people are just not really clear on what their goal is. More questions required! The most important thing you can do to help your team member when they're unclear is to ask more questions to reveal a clear goal. Until you do this there is no point in moving on to the next step. If they're not clear on where they're headed then there is no way you're going to be able to help them figure out how they might get there. Think about it like trying to book flights for a holiday when you don't know where you're flying to. It doesn't really work, does it?

Have a look at the GROW question bank on page 228 to find some great questions to help you start uncovering your team member's goal.

Reality

So, if your team member's goal is Point B, then their reality is Point A. It's the current situation or their current reality. Where are they now? Again, using our simple holiday analogy – we've figured out that we're flying to London (that's our goal) but where are we departing from? In other words, where are we now? Depending on whether we're leaving from Sydney or New York the journey is going to be very different, isn't it?

One of the fascinating things about asking questions around the current situation is that sometimes the team member discovers that while initially they thought they were in Sydney, after a few questions they realise that they're actually in Hawaii! More often than not, this is a pleasant discovery – they realise that they're further along the path to the destination than they thought and of course this alters the journey that they're going to take.

Have a look at the GROW question bank on page 228 to find some great questions to help you start uncovering your team member's current reality.

Often when a team member reaches out to you with a, 'Hey, do you have five minutes … ?' and you think, 'Oh, what's happened … ?', they start talking to you about the current reality. They don't start with the Goal. They tell you what's happening right now and the challenge or issue that they're facing, and you can ask some great questions there to help them get really clear and then you will have to take them back to the Goal. It might sound something like this:

> Okay Jen. That sounds like a pretty tricky situation you're in. And what specifically would you like to achieve instead?

Spending time in the Goal and Reality sections is important. Don't move forward to the next step until the team member is really clear on their Goal (where they want to get to) and their Reality (where they are right now). If you move forward before clarity is achieved it will be really difficult to identify options, so if you find your team member struggling to generate options you may find it helpful to revisit the Goal or Reality sections again.

Options

Okay, so your team member is flying to London and they're in Hawaii now – what might be the best flight options to get there? This is where options come in. I always feel like the Options step is like a mini brainstorm. You're asking questions and your team member is generating as many possible options as they can in relation to achieving their goal. As with any brainstorming session, don't evaluate the options in the beginning, just enable your team member to generate as many as they can.

Have a look at the GROW question bank on page 228 to find some great questions to help your team member generate options.

When the options come out in rapid succession you can be certain that your team member has more options in the tank. Ask, '… and what else?', and see what else they can come up with. If the pace of options starts to slow down that's an indicator that the tank may be starting to empty. 'And what else?' is placed at the centre of the question bank as it is appropriate to use it in every stage of the GROW model. When your team member thinks that they are done, I love to ask one final question: 'If there was one more thing you could do, perhaps a bit left field, what might that be?' You'll be amazed at the ideas people will come up with, often this last option can be gold as your team member starts thinking a bit laterally.

As their leader you might think that they've missed an option or that there might be a huge risk with one of the options. But sit tight for now and trust the process of GROW – as you work through the evaluation of options stage, these things may arise anyway – trust your team member to do the work – and if they don't then you could always bring it to their attention before you move on to the next stage. As you begin to use GROW, I would strongly encourage you to resist adding in your ideas all the time. Your mission is to see what great work your team member can come up with by themselves and support them in their learning. I talk about this more at the end of the chapter in the 'What if?' section, and show you what resisting might look like. And of course, I hope it goes without saying that if you see that they might be placing themselves or others inadvertently in danger, either physically or psychologically, you would call that out straight away. Our number one commitment to our team must always be to keep them safe and healthy.

So, with that said, once your team member has a solid list of options to choose from you can start asking questions to help them evaluate which options might be the best to move forward with. Which one will best meet the goal?

Once your team member has selected a great option you can move into the final stage: Wrap up.

Wrap up

The wrap up component is very important. This is where your team member identifies what specifically they are going to do, by when and what, if any, additional support they may need. If you don't get very detailed in this area about what your team member is specifically going to do to take action on this issue, all you will have had is a nice conversation about their challenge.

If we continue our holiday analogy, your team member has selected one particular flight, so now what do they need to do? Well, they need to book it! And they might need to check if their passport is valid, figure out whether they need a visa, they might need to get some foreign currency and they need to pack. And all of this needs to be done prior to the departure date. The wrap up step often looks like a mini action plan.

Have a look at the GROW question bank on page 228 to find some great questions to support your team member to wrap up their actions really specifically.

Now you've learned the four components of GROW – Goal, Reality, Options, Wrap Up – you can use powerful questions to enable your team members to solve their own problems. Having this structure at your fingertips prevents you from jumping in with advice when your team member is perfectly capable of solving their problems by themselves.

Set yourself a wee challenge! See how often you can enable your team members to solve their own problems *without* providing any advice or your own solutions. And remember, you're taking a *coaching approach* to supporting your team member to resolve their problems. This means that when an alarm bell goes off in your head, while you can certainly share that with your team member, there is a great way to do that, which involves flipping your concerns or advice into questions. We'll cover that in the challenges section that follows.

GROW question bank

Goal

What is it you would like to discuss?

What's on your mind?
What is your immediate goal?
What would be your ideal scenario?

What do you want?
What is the result or outcome you want?
What would you like to happen that is not happening now?
And what will happen if you achieve that?
On a scale of 1 to 10, how important is that issue to you?

Reality

What is the situation right now?
What keeps you up at night?

What's the real challenge here for you?
In the current situation, what are others saying?
What is it about the situation that you don't want?
How often does this happen?
What effect does this have?
What else is relevant?
Who else is relevant?
What is their perception of the situation?
Given what we've discussed are there any refinements you would like to make to your goal? (If yes, go back to Goal)

Options

What are your options?
What other possibilities for action do you see?
And what's another approach?
If our roles were reversed, what would you tell me to do?

If you're saying yes to this, what are you saying no to?
What approach/actions have you seen used, or used yourself, in similar circumstances?
What criteria would you use to judge the options?
Which one seems the best fit?
What are the benefits of that option?
And what would be the consequence of that?

Wrap up

What are you most excited about doing?
How can you keep track of results?
What might get in the way?
What do you need to do to overcome that?
Who or what do you need to support you?

What help do you need from me?
What are the next steps?
Precisely, when will you take them?
What is it that you are going to do?
How will I know that you've done it?

What was the most useful learning here for you?

(Center: *And what else?*)

* Michael Bungay Stanier has identified the seven questions he believes are most useful when you're learning to coach which he sets out in his book, *The Coaching Habit*. They are included here in italics.

WHAT IFS: COMMON CHALLENGES AND HOW TO OVERCOME THEM

What if I can see a problem or an opportunity to solve the problem that my team member is unaware of?

This often happens when – given your knowledge and experience – you might see a 'land mine' that your team member is about to put their foot on which they cannot see at all. How do you bring this to their attention without simply yelling out, 'Don't step there! There's a land mine!' After all, we want our team to be able to start spotting land mines for themselves. If we always have to be the spotter, they will never be able to go anywhere without us. (*And that's BAD!*)

So, let's look at a situation where there's a risk in the way your team member wants to move forward that they can't see. It might go something like this.

Let's imagine your team member is working in a finance team and is trying to pull together information from different areas of the business to provide a report to the executive team, but one area still hasn't provided their information after several email reminders. You're in the thick of the 'Options' part of the GROW conversation:

Team Member: … So what I think I'll do is I'll just escalate this straight to their manager and let them know that this team still hasn't delivered their information to me and they can sort them out.

Leader: Yes, that's definitely an option. (*Thinking *I can see that this might damage the relationship between my team member and the person in the finance team – how might we avoid this?*)* If you proceed with that option, what do you think might be the consequences of that?

Team Member: Well, I'll probably get my data quicker!

Leader: Yes, possibly. And what else might happen?

Team Member: Hmmmm. Well, they might be a bit grumpy that I didn't have a conversation with them directly and just went straight to their leader ... they might feel that I've got them into trouble. Hmmmm, I didn't really think about that.

Leader: Okay, that sounds like a bit of a risk. How might you handle that a bit differently to maintain your relationship with them AND get your data?

Team Member: Well maybe I should go and sit down with them and make sure they're really clear about what I need and why, and what the consequences might be if I don't have their data for the executive meeting. And also, I can find out if they need any support from me to deliver on my request. I might even ask them if there's any support they need from their leader to deliver the data.

Leader: That sounds like a great way to do it. Anything else you need from me ... ?

And now let's compare the conversation above, which uses a coaching approach to resolving problems, to the alternative of just simply giving advice:

Team Member: ... So what I think I'll do is I'll just escalate this straight to their manager and let them know that this team still hasn't delivered their information to me and they can sort them out.

Leader: No, don't do that. Just go and talk to them directly and make sure they're really clear what you need and why, and what the consequences might be if you don't have their data.

The difference is stark, isn't it? No learning opportunity in the second version, and your team member has walked away with the message that they were 'wrong' and that you are 'right' and that they need to keep coming back to you to make sure they don't make mistakes. Boooooo!

And what if despite your exceptional questions, the team member still hasn't identified the 'land mine'? Well of course you can share that with them, but make sure you've exhausted their own thinking first. Using the question '… and what else?' a few times is a great way to keep stretching your team member to come up with more options or suggestions before you add in your own observations. If you can stick with it and trust the '… and what else?' question, you'll rarely have to resort to giving advice.

What if my team member thinks they're always right, even when they're wrong?

If you find yourself in this situation with a team member, flick back to the previous chapter's 'What If' section and read the response to 'What if my team member says they have nothing to learn?'

DRA learning reflection

Discoveries:

- As a leader you now enable your team to solve their own problems; you don't solve them for them.
- The GROW model is a useful tool you can use to help your people solve their own problems.
- When you work on G for Goal, you're supporting the discovery of the actual challenge or outcome sought.
- When you work on R for Reality, you're supporting the discovery of where your team member is currently now.
- When you work on O for Options, you're supporting the generation of potential options to achieve the goal.
- When you work on W for Wrap Up, you're supporting the identification of concrete next steps.
- You need to switch from providing answers to offering questions.

Reflection questions:

- On a scale of 1 to 10, with 1 low and 10 high, to what extent does your desk resemble the deli counter at your local supermarket? (*Take a number, please!*)
- What might your team members say about your ability to support them in solving their own problems?
- How frequently do you solve problems for your team without asking them for any suggestions or recommendations first?

- Who do you know that asks really good questions that make you think deeply? What kind of questions do they ask? How do you feel when you work with them?
- Who do you know that asks few questions and mainly offers their own opinion and suggestions? How do you feel when you work with them?
- What could you do more of, if your team were resolving their problems for themselves?

Actions to choose from:
- When my team members come to me with a problem, instead of telling them the answer, I will use the GROW model to help them solve the problem themselves.
- When my team members ask me for advice, instead of giving them the advice straight away, I will ask them, 'What suggestions do you have?'
- When my team members have lots of suggestions, instead of dropping in my opinion or advice, I will ask '… and what else?' to draw out further suggestions.

'Success is nothing more than a few simple disciplines practiced every day.'

Jim Rohn

Chapter 14

CREATING YOUR VERY OWN PEOPLE LEADERSHIP DEVELOPMENT PLAN

Now that you've read through the book and popped out on the other side it's time to pull everything together into your development plan. Development, as we've discussed, is critical to your success. And like anything that's worth doing well, it's worth creating a really good plan.

If you've read through the book and realised that you're in the fortunate position where you have an exceptional people leader who is genuinely invested in developing you and together you have already crafted a solid leadership development plan, that's great! You may like to use this section as a 'quality check' on your plan to see if it could benefit from any fine tuning.

If your people leader is more inexperienced, or perhaps your organisation isn't quite firing on all cylinders when it comes to people development, maybe you need a little more help.

As you know I am personally invested in your success, and I want to help you as much as I can. Jump to our bonus resources page at the back of the book to download our free development plan template. This template will help you distil your thinking, capture your development opportunity, apply your learning and create a five-star development plan you can be really proud of.

Let's get into it ...

IDENTIFY YOUR DEVELOPMENT OPPORTUNITIES

As you've progressed through the book, any opportunities you have should have come to your attention. And if there weren't any areas for improvement between the leader you want to become and where you are now – congratulations! – there's no development to do. Job done. Shut the book. And r-e-l-a-x. Or if you're keen, perhaps you might ask yourself the question: how could I develop my leadership *further*? Then some additional opportunities may emerge.

But, for most of us, when we reflect on who we want to be and where we are now, there will likely be, at the very least, a few rough edges that we can polish and some gaps to fill. If not, the odd one or two deep crevasses. Use the chapter summaries to identify your key areas for development:

- What are your initial thoughts around your development areas?

IDENTIFY YOUR DEVELOPMENT PRIORITY

So, you've identified your opportunities. Awesome! Now what ... ? After you've done your analysis of your development needs and have listed all your areas for improvement, there is a risk that you charge off into the sunset, guns blazing, with your 54 development opportunities and ... get lost! Behaviour change is hard, it taxes the brain as you go through this rewiring process, and therefore I strongly recommend that you start with a really manageable number of development priorities.

Let's say ... one. No, I'm not kidding. One is a really good number. Which one is your priority and why?

It doesn't mean that you chuck out the other 53. All it means is that you look at your list of development opportunities and prioritise them. Which one is *most* important to focus on to develop my people leadership right now and why? Having a compelling 'why' will make you far more likely to persist with this opportunity. Start with that one.

As an example you might choose:

> To improve my coaching skills so that I can enable my team to achieve their goals.

GENERATE ACTIONS AND RELEVANT HABITS

Now that you've selected your priority, think about some actions that could help you move forward.

Using our example above, some actions might be:

- Read coaching and leadership books.
- Improve my listening skills.
- Ask for coaching from my leader.
- Focus on asking open and targeted questions.
- Encourage my team members to give me feedback for improvement.

These actions sound good, but they're much more useful when we turn them into a developmental habit. (Flick back to page 14 in chapter 1 if you need a wee refresher on how to build a habit.)

Let's take action number 1: Read coaching and leadership books, and turn that into a habit:

> When I'm having lunch each day (triggering event) instead of picking up my phone to check social media (stop doing) I will read five pages – *or a chapter if you're keen* – of *The Coaching Habit* (start doing).

You may feel confident to implement a few new behaviours at a time in relation to your development priority; just remember to take your time. Then when you have habituated that behaviour (you can do it without thinking) then just select the next one from your list, and so on. I think one overarching development priority per quarter *may* be about right, depending of course on the complexity of the priority you've chosen and how much time you've set aside for practice.

ASK FOR SUPPORT

Once you've selected your development priority and created your new habits then ask for support from those around you. Who specifically might you ask to support you with your development? Call on your support crew – that's what they're there for. They can offer you support in a number of ways, including providing encouragement as you try new things, providing an accountability loop to ensure you keep persevering, providing feedback to let you know how you're going, and possibly even challenging you at times. If you're really lucky they may even coach you. Woohoooo!

The other interesting thing about asking for help from your support crew on your number one development priority is that now they know what you're doing – you have effectively made a commitment to them, and this single act can spur you on to achieve your development goal.

SET ASIDE TIME FOR PRACTICE AND REFLECTION

Remember in chapter 1 we talked about learning how to learn? We covered reading, reflection, journalling and habit development. Now you need to use these tools to support you with your number one development priority. Block out time in your calendar for both practice and reflection. When are you going to practise and with whom? When will you reflect? What gets scheduled gets done. Don't put it on a 'to do list', block time into your diary. Go on, lock in some time now and you will already be on the path to success. You got this!

ENLIST YOUR TEAM

When you share with your team what you're working on, guess what? They will hold up the mirror to you whenever you're not doing what you said.

Painful, yet helpful. Hopefully they will also congratulate and encourage you when you're doing well. Either way you're engaging them on your development journey. You're saying, 'I have learning to do, and you can help.' How empowering is that? And look at you now, you're leading. It really is a beautiful thing.

'Becoming isn't about arriving somewhere or achieving a certain aim. It's forward motion, a means of evolving, a way to reach continuously toward a better self.'

Michelle Obama

NEXT STEPS

Well, here we are. At the beginning.

'But isn't this the end of the book?!' I hear you question under your breath.

And we're both right. It *is* the end of the book – and it's the beginning of the next exciting chapter of your people leadership practice.

Firstly, I want to thank you sincerely for investing your precious time in your personal growth and development as a people leader. I'm confident your team is going to thank you even more. And quite possibly your family will thank you too. When you develop your people leadership capabilities it has a lovely way of flowing outside our workspaces and into our homes – consider it extra value on your investment! I hope you made lots of exciting and thought-provoking discoveries and had some brain-zapping reflections and a-ha moments too. Perhaps you received some helpful reminders to keep doing some good things that you've done in the past, but that had inadvertently fallen by the wayside. And how did you go with your habits? Have you identified some habits that you can start to put in place? Yes? Awesome. So, you've completed your reading, now it's time to put it into practice.

As you begin these new practices, I urge you to start really small. Just take a teensy, tiny step – implement one habit from your development plan – and just do that one thing every day until you have it down pat and you can do it without even thinking. Then, and only then, select the next one. When you implement one habit at a time you will ignite a tiny spark which before you know it becomes a warm and sustaining inner fire which fuels your people leadership growth.

Finally, no-one is going to be a leader quite like you. I've provided you with a framework that you can use and some wisdom to get you started. Your mission is to take the framework and make it your own. You have a unique combination of wisdom, talents and experience; use the framework to leverage your strengths, bring insight to your challenges and enable you to be and do better.

I believe in you. I know you can do this. So, I'll ask one last time; are you up for it? I hope that was a 'Hell yes!'

Right. I'm not into long farewells (having spent way too much time crying in international airport departure lounges over the years) so it's time for you to get going. Get on your marks, get set, and LEAD! Show me the inspiring and enabling leader you can become.

To a Louse, On Seeing One on a Lady's Bonnet, At Church

Robert Burns

Burns original

Ha! whaur ye gaun, ye crowlin ferlie?
Your impudence protects you sairly;
I canna say but ye strunt rarely,
Owre gauze and lace;
Tho', faith! I fear ye dine but sparely
On sic a place.

Ye ugly, creepin, blastit wonner,
Detested, shunn'd by saunt an' sinner,
How daur ye set your fit upon her-
Sae fine a lady?
Gae somewhere else and seek your dinner
On some poor body.

Swith! in some beggar's haffet squattle;
There ye may creep, and sprawl, and sprattle,
Wi' ither kindred, jumping cattle,
In shoals and nations;
Whaur horn nor bane ne'er daur unsettle
Your thick plantations.

Now haud you there, ye're out o' sight,
Below the fatt'rels, snug and tight;
Na, faith ye yet! ye'll no be right,
Till ye've got on it-
The verra tapmost, tow'rin height
O' Miss' bonnet.

My sooth! right bauld ye set your nose out,
As plump an' grey as ony groset:

O for some rank, mercurial rozet,
Or fell, red smeddum,
I'd gie you sic a hearty dose o't,
Wad dress your droddum.

I wad na been surpris'd to spy
You on an auld wife's flainen toy;
Or aiblins some bit dubbie boy,
On's wyliecoat;
But Miss' fine Lunardi! fye!
How daur ye do't?

O Jeany, dinna toss your head,
An' set your beauties a' abread!
Ye little ken what cursed speed
The blastie's makin:
Thae winks an' finger-ends, I dread,
Are notice takin.

O wad some Power the giftie gie us
To see oursels as ithers see us!
It wad frae mony a blunder free us,
An' foolish notion:
What airs in dress an' gait wad lea'e us,
An' ev'n devotion!

Standard English translation of the final verse

Oh, would some Power give us the gift
To see ourselves as others see us!
It would from many a blunder free us,
And foolish notion:
What airs in dress and gait would leave us,
And even devotion!

RECOMMENDED READING

Throughout this book you will have noticed a sprinkling of other texts worthy of your attention. They are included again here for your easy reference. I've categorised them by subject so if you find an area you want to stretch in you know what to read. I have also added some extra books into the list which, from my experience, will add depth to your leadership knowledge and understanding as you learn and grow. This is absolutely *not* an exhaustive list; simply some prompts to get you moving and fuel your learning.

Remember you can listen to books as you commute or exercise. It's such an easy way to develop yourself and the *only* form of multi-tasking I actually condone! Or if you prefer you can download them onto your favourite e-reader or, like me, buy the printed book. I LOVE books!

Enjoy!

Coaching and resolving problems
- *The Coaching Habit: Say less, ask more and change the way you lead forever*, Michael Bungay Stanier
- *The Advice Trap: Be humble, stay curious and change the way you lead forever*, Michael Bungay Stanier
- *The Miracle of Mindfulness: The classic guide*, Thich Nhat Hanh
- *Coaching for Performance: The principles and practice of coaching and leadership*, Sir John Whitmore and Performance Consultants

- *EXTRA: The Third Space: Using life's little transitions to find balance and happiness*, Dr Adam Fraser

Connection
- *Emotional Intelligence: Why it can matter more than IQ*, Daniel Goleman
- *The Mindful Leader: 7 Practices for transforming your leadership, your organisation and your life*, Michael Bunting
- *Quiet: The power of introverts in a world that can't stop talking*, Susan Cain

Communication
- *You're not Listening: What you're missing and why it matters*, Kate Murphy
- *Conversational Intelligence: How great leaders build trust and get extraordinary results*, Judith Glaser
- *EXTRA: Crucial Conversations: Tools for talking when stakes are high*, Kerry Patterson, Joseph Grenny, Ron McMillan, Al Switzler

Development
- *The 7 Habits of Highly Effective People*, Steven Covey
- *The Ideal Team Player: How to recognise and cultivate the three essential virtues*, Patrick Lencioni
- *EXTRA: The Five Dysfunctions of a Team: A leadership fable*, Patrick Lencioni

Focus
- *Switch: How to change things when change is hard*, Chip Heath and Dan Heath
- *The Advantage: Why organisational health trumps everything else in business*, Patrick Lencioni
- *Start with Why: How great leaders inspire everyone to take action*, Simon Sinek

Habits
- *Atomic Habits: An easy and proven way to build good habits and break bad ones*, James Clear
- *EXTRA: The Power of Habit: Why we do what we do, and how to change*, Charles Duhigg
- *EXTRA: Tiny Habits: Why starting small makes lasting change easy*, BJ Fogg PhD

Learning
- *Man's Search for Meaning*, Viktor E. Frankl
- *Mindset: Changing the way you think to fulfil your potential*, Carol Dweck
- *EXTRA: Think Again: The power of knowing what you don't know*, Adam Grant

But wait, there's more!
- *The Celestine Prophecy: An adventure*, James Redfield
- *Dare to Lead: Daring greatly and rising strong at work*, Brené Brown
- *Leaders Eat Last: Why some teams pull together and some don't*, Simon Sinek
- *Who Moved my Cheese? An amazing way to deal with change in your work and in your life*, Dr Spencer Johnson

BONUS RESOURCES

If you've turned to this page to access the free resources I'm delighted, as it means you want to implement your learnings and take action to become an even better people leader. Woop!

There are two free downloadable resources:

Simple Development Process Overview

If you'd like an easy-to-follow process to set yourself and your organisation up for success and you'd like to ditch the annual 'tick and flick exercise' for good, have I got the process for you! Use this process to have engaging development conversations with your team members.

Leadership Development Plan template

If you're ready to distil your thinking, capture your development opportunities, apply your learnings and have a five-star development plan you can be really proud of, this is the template for you. This plan will help you get your habits on so you can become your very best.

Ready to dig in?

Simply scan the QR code to download these resources or find out more at www.peoplemastery.com/lead.

HEARTFELT THANKS AND APPRECIATION

Deepest love and special thanks to my family. Writing a book takes a lot of time and even more perseverance. Thank you, Anthony, for creating the space for me to do the work and for picking up and so beautifully managing all the balls I dropped at home along the way. Thanks also for being my biggest fan and for lovingly building my confidence over the many wonderful years we've been together to the point where I believed that I could do this. You are the best covert coach and staunchest supporter ever. I also learn so much about my leadership from leading two very special members of our home team: Neve and Miles. Thank you Neve and Miles for all the rich experiences we have shared together. You provide so many opportunities for my learning and growth, and I hope I return the favour! I hope you enjoy seeing some of our stories in this book. Thanks for your loving patience and encouragement as I spent hours writing. The three of you are always on my mind and in my heart.

Special shout out to the first team I was ever involved in: The Jackson Family team. Thanks Mum and Dad for developing me and showing me what good leadership looks like from a very young age. And thanks to Fenwick, Eve and Helen for countless lessons in team dynamics!

My People Mastery Gals; Ash, Bec, JD, Jen, Kirsty and Kristi. Susannah,

I consider you a surrogate PM team member too! Wow, so grateful for each and every one of you. Supportive, caring, kind, encouraging, inspiring, and the list goes on! It has been the hardest thing *not* sharing the content of the book with you all along the way. That said, each and every one of you have shaped who I am as a leader and how I lead, so I hope you will see and feel your contributions in the book. In particular JD, loving gratitude for your mentorship through the many years we have worked together and the wonderful DRA cycle that we now know and love; another of your great ideas! I'm grateful that we all champion one another's learning and I thank you all for your enduring support during this particular development journey.

Andrew Griffiths; the best book coach a gal could ever wish for. Thanks so much Andrew for creating a warm and supportive environment, as well as a kick ass structure, for me to write this book. Thanks also to Bron, my writing partner in crime, for your encouragement and friendly nudges along the way. I feel very lucky that we had Andrew's full attention in our dynamic duo book writing program.

Thanks to Michael Hanrahan, Anna Clemann and the 'behind-the-scenes' team at Publish Central for their extensive publishing and book design expertise – I always felt in such safe hands. I'll never forget your supportive email Michael with Kermit the Frog wildly typing on his typewriter, your humour always arrived at just the right time. I'm sure the book cover design was specifically timed to get me through the challenging episode of 'not quite at final manuscript stage'. Thanks, Anna, for providing 'colour and movement' to keep me going!

Thank you also to the fabulously talented Melinda Hird for taking awesome pictures, including the one on the back of this book, and making me look (and feel) like a superstar. I certainly wouldn't have scrubbed up so well without the makeup magic of Helen Sotiropoulos. Thanks Helen. The photos don't convey how much time and creative effort goes into taking a shot that is 'just right'. You nailed it! Thank you, Mel and Helen.

What would I have done without my book buddy, my trail blazer, my support and guide? Not much! I learnt so much from watching you ahead of me on the book writing trail, Kirsty. Thank you for your time, your loving support and your constant encouragement and reassurance.

They say it takes a village to raise a family and I'd argue it also takes a village to write a book. It's the early morning breakfast catch ups, the chats over a cup of tea, the power walks, the phone calls, the supportive 'thinking of you' text messages, the 'I'll have the kids', and everything else that makes a difference every single day. Thank you to my favourite fairy godmother, beautiful friends and extended family for your encouragement and support of me and mine. Every gesture, no matter how small, made a difference. Thank you.

Thanks also to my previous team members, leaders and colleagues for providing such rich experiences that I have the benefit of drawing on now. You have all contributed to shape the leader I have become and I hope I have shared these learnings in a way that also enables others to benefit from your collective wisdom – paying it forward, so to speak. Special mention to Chyonne Kreltszheim for introducing to me to the work of Jim Rohn and most especially for creating the coaching moment where I 'discovered' that there's no evidence to suggest I can't do the work I do.

Thank you to Anny Druett for her engaging and illuminating training on Australia's First Nations people – such important work.

Very special thanks to (in order of appearance) Steve Anderson, Neill Emmett, Sharon Hansen, Sharon Howes, Chip McFarlane, Dr Hilary Armstrong, Kate Jackson, Julie Murthy, Kirsty Salvestro, Michael Taggart, Jillian Ackary Dirou, Anthony Marshall, Rachel Dibley, Brett Jones and Shane Gill for their positive influence on my leadership and for granting me permission to share their stories and their names in this book. I'm thrilled that I can share your positivity with everyone who reads this book. Thank you.

And finally, I have deep gratitude to my clients. I learn so much from you and with you and I hope you all feel the same way about me and my fabulous People Mastery team. I continue to be bowled over by your willingness to step into the discomfort of new things and lean into the learning. I value your experiences and your stories, the good, the bad, the ugly and the funny, and your generosity in sharing them all with me. I hope this book respectfully reflects our journeys together.

Heartfelt thanks to you all.

READY FOR A WEE BIT MORE...?

More leadership development?
More learnings?
More inspiration and support?
(Or even a wee bit more Scottish accent? C'mon, you know you are!)

If you're feeling inspired after reading *On Your Marks, Get Set... LEAD!* and would like to boost your learning even more, there are a number of ways you can work with Anna and the team at People Mastery. Check out the information on the following pages and visit www.peoplemastery.com/lead.

You can also keep the inspiration coming your way by following Anna on LinkedIn.

DiSC PROFILE & 1:1 DEBRIEF

Find out what makes you and others tick – and supercharge your relationship-building skills – with this personalised, in-depth profile and virtual debrief session with Anna or another accredited DiSC practitioner within the People Mastery team.

Includes:

- ✓ 20-page DiSC Profile + Supplement Report
- ✓ 1 hour personal virtual debrief with a DiSC Practitioner
- ✓ Podcast about your style
- ✓ A 3-step process to identify other people's DiSC styles
- ✓ Additional online resources

Ready to begin your journey with DiSC? Scan the QR code to get started or find out more at www.peoplemastery.com/lead.

LEADERSHIP COACHING

Accelerate your journey toward achieving your potential with Anna or another People Mastery accredited and experienced coach. Identify your strengths and opportunities, overcome challenges and grow your skills and confidence.

Includes:

- ✓ 6 × 1 hour tailored sessions with your coach
- ✓ A formal leadership development plan
- ✓ Additional online resources

Book your free coaching discovery conversation by scanning the QR code or check out 1-on-1 coaching at www.peoplemastery.com/lead.

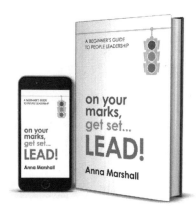

READY FOR A RICH DISCUSSION? JOIN US FOR BOOK GROUP

Join us for a series of facilitated highly interactive discussions to take a deeper dive into the key concepts from *On Your Marks, Get Set … LEAD!* Gain new insights and boost your ability to embed new leadership practices. Includes:

✓ 4 × 1-hour virtual sessions
✓ Small groups (max. 8 people) for highly interactive discussion
✓ Building a new network with diverse, yet like-minded individuals
✓ Additional online resources

Register for Book Group by scanning the QR code or check out Book Groups at www.peoplemastery.com/lead.

YOU'VE READ THE BOOK NOW ENROL IN THE 'LEAD!' ONLINE PROGRAM

This comprehensive, highly interactive, self-paced online program will take you from 'theory' to 'practice' in a flash. Guaranteed to boost your real-life leadership skills!

Includes:

- ✓ Online program
- ✓ Choose-your-own-adventure style leadership scenarios
- ✓ Quizzes and activities
- ✓ Downloadable program workbook
- ✓ Leadership development plan
- ✓ And more …

Book your free program discovery conversation by scanning the QR code or check out the 'LEAD!' program at www.peoplemastery.com/lead.

WOULD YOU LIKE TO INTERVIEW ANNA?

Anna brings a distinctive blend of energy, enthusiasm and optimism into her work. Be warned – it's infectious! Her passion is to inspire people and enable them to flourish. Anna is happy to be interviewed for a feature in your publication, for your podcast or live for television or radio.

Anna can engage your audience on the following topics:

✓ Developing 'coaching leaders'
✓ Creating values-led, performance-enabling cultures
✓ Building cohesive teams
✓ Breaking down silos in organisations

If you would like to interview Anna about her book *On Your Marks, Get Set ... LEAD!* or any of the topics above, please scan the QR code or email hello@peoplemastery.com.

LOOKING FOR THE PERFECT GIFT FOR YOUR FIRST-TIME PEOPLE LEADERS?

What better way to support your leaders than by gifting them a copy of this book? It's a perfect support for your leaders who:

- ✓ Are keen to make the transition from technical expert to people leader
- ✓ Have just been appointed as leaders for the first time
- ✓ Are participating in formal leadership development activities
- ✓ Are keen to BE and DO more as first-time people leaders
- ✓ Are leading other people leaders and need a 'refresh' (*you know what we're saying here, right?*)

Some other ideas:

- ✓ Pop into welcome packs for new leaders to your business
- ✓ Include as a resource for your Leader development program
- ✓ Send as a Thank you or recognition gift
- ✓ Use as gifts at Awards ceremonies

If you would like to buy copies of the book in bulk for your organisation, and/or signed and personalised copies by the author, please scan the QR code or email hello@peoplemastery.com.